RICH BY CHOICE

POOR BY HABIT

For Ashley,
May all your
choices be spicy.
Yours in
love and dance,

Thanks for
tapping with
me. You're
terrific!

2-07

Copyright © 2004 by Laurie Johnson

Edited by: Belinda Perez
Art Direction: Francisco E. Cervantes, DG Pen
Illustrations: Martin Cantú
Layout and Design: Fine Line Design 204.755.2239
Cover Photography: Dennis Mukai
Cover Design: Dennis Serras

For my mother, Adele, a constant source of encouragement in my life.
For my big brother Kevin, I love you.
For my true friend, Belinda, the "Mastermind".

In loving memory of Flossie Johnson.

CONTENTS

Acknowledgements   vii
Introduction   ix

BOOK ONE – LIFE MANAGEMENT

Rich Choices vs. Poor Habits   **3**

Break a Habit Before It Breaks You   **11**
  A LAURIE STORY – In High School I Proved to Myself
  I Could Fail. In College I Proved to Myself I Could Succeed.
  ACTIVITY – We Are What We Repeatedly Do!

Personal Goal Setting   **19**
  A LAURIE STORY – Inch by Inch It's a Cinch!
  ACTIVITY – Step Into the Future!

"Tap In" to Your Full Potential   **25**
  A LAURIE STORY – I'm Committed and I'm Unstoppable.
  ANOTHER LAURIE STORY – What Do the Hula
  Hoop and Lotus 123 Have in Common?
  ACTIVITY – Commitment is Great!

Always Do Your Best   **33**
  A LAURIE STORY – Measure Twice, Cut Once!
  ACTIVITY – Is That Your Best Work?

It's Your Body – Protect It, Respect It   **41**
  A LAURIE STORY – The Writing's on the Wall!
  ACTIVITY – Your Future is Self-Determined!

Your Thinking Creates Your Reality   **53**
  A LAURIE STORY – A Bad Attitude or a Bad Day?
  ACTIVITY – What Do Your Thoughts Say About You?

The Clock is Ticking –Intelligent Time Management   **61**
  A LAURIE STORY – How Long Does It Take to Write a Book?
  ACTIVITY – Procrastination – This Can't Wait!

CONTENTS

Opportunity, Courage, Fear and Risk   71

    A LAURIE STORY – The Gregory Hines Story:
When Courage and Opportunity Meet!
ANOTHER LAURIE STORY – My Experience on the
John Walsh Show: I Think I'm Afraid!
ACTIVITY – Pull Yourself Together!

Got Forgiveness   83

    A LAURIE STORY – Forgiveness – The Antidote to Anger!
ACTIVITY – No More Resistance!

Relationship Inventory   91

    A LAURIE STORY – Running with the Big Dogs!
ACTIVITY – Mapping Your Social World!

Design Your Life With Passion   99

    A LAURIE STORY – Tapping Into Wealth: How I
Turned My Passion for Tap Dancing Into a Career!
ACTIVITY – Are You Passionate?

Laurie's Passion Principles   111

    A LAURIE STORY – Go Ahead,
Tell Me I Don't Have What It Takes!
ACTIVITY – Your Passion Fashion!

BOOK TWO – FINANCIAL MANAGEMENT

Financial Goal Setting   123

    A LAURIE STORY – Change is Good!
ACTIVITY – My Financial Goals!

Right on the Money – Successful Budgeting   131

    A LAURIE STORY – I Was Broke, But I Wasn't Poor!
ACTIVITY – Budgeting – Making Ends Meet!

CONTENTS

Intelligent Consumption   143
A LAURIE STORY – I Got Booted!
ACTIVITY – Your Values – Ch-ching, Ch-ching, Ch-ching!

Stop Spending, Start Saving   153
A LAURIE STORY – Pobody's Nerfect!
ACTIVITY – No More Cash in the Trash, Please!

Credit Card Management   161
A LAURIE STORY – The Credit Card Blues!
ACTIVITY – Are You Credit Worthy? The Credit Card Quiz!

Checking Accounts   179
A LAURIE STORY – Everything Checks Out – Almost!
ACTIVITY – The Balancing Act!

Time is Money   187
A LAURIE STORY – Penny Power!
ACTIVITY – Strategizing!

The Big Payback – Investing 101   195
A LAURIE STORY – Wake Up and Mix It Up!
ACTIVITY – Ten Years from Now…

The Roth IRA   205
A LAURIE STORY – No Drama to Report!
ACTIVITY – What? It's Mine and It's Tax Free?

Protecting Yourself from Identity Theft and Fraud   211
A LAURIE STORY – I Do What I Can to Protect My SSN!
ACTIVITY – Where are Your V.I.P.'s (Very Important Paper's)?

Life Commitments   220

Financial Commitments   221

Stop dreaming! Decide what you want and…   223

ACKNOWLEDGEMENTS

I wish to acknowledge and thank the following people for their support and encouragement: Julie Adler, Sharmell 'Day' Brown, Sidney Brown, Lola Holman Blank (lhbentertainment.com), Catherine and Al Dixon, Elena Galvez, Pam Graham, Acia Grey, Emily Jackson, Kevin Johnson, Mary Johnson (imaginetheimpossible.org), Shelli K. Margheritis (skmsolutions.com), Sarah Anindo Marshall, Joelle Martinec, Lee Moczygemba (amertraining.com), Caitlin Morais (gislounge.com), Christine Nelson, Harvey Newkirk, Belinda Perez (govmanage.com), Vicente J. and Imelda B. Perez, Vincent Perez (vvstyle.com), Diane and Eric Ratley, Joe Tremaine, Essy Waldrop and Michael Waldrop (twofortap.com), and Mark Yamarone.

To my nieces and nephews, I thank you for your inspiration. I hope this book saves you a lot of D-R-A-M-A!

INTRODUCTION

Most men die at age 25 but are not buried until they are 70.

— *Benjamin Franklin*

I travel around the country speaking to audiences of all ages. When addressing elementary school kids, they are excited about their futures. "I want to be a politician" shouts one student. "I'm going to start my own computer software company building games," adds another. "I want to be a dancer," claims a third. When I talk with junior high school students, visions and dreams of the future are less vivid. Sadly, half the audience admits to not having any!

By the time students are in high school or college, many of their dreams have faded. It's as if the thought never crossed their minds. Dreams? Goals? Why bother? Only a few students in this age group can state their goals. Adult audiences are even more disheartening, usually only one or two individuals can state their dreams. What happened? Why does our passion for the future fade and die as we go through life?

I have found that by the time most people become adults they are doubtful, hopeless, fearful, and negative. Self-doubt, coupled with limited, small-time thinking has become a habit and a way of life. They've given up on themselves and their dreams, and are working at dead-end jobs they detest. The result is a painful life spent in "survival mode."

Don't become someone who struggles simply to survive and yet, barely does so. There is no passion and no meaning living in "survival mode." Living in survival mode means you unenthusiastically crawl out of bed, grudgingly prepare for the day, reluctantly rush off to work or school, drag yourself home, halfheartedly prepare dinner, watch television, pass out, and then repeat the whole process the following day. It's no surprise there is no passion and no meaning. You're sleepwalking through life!

Designing a life based on your passions is not easy, but it is necessary. Regardless of what you want to create for your life, build it on a foundation of integrity, honesty, and excellence.

Rich by Choice, Poor by Habit is a concise and easy-to-understand guide to some of the most powerful, life-enriching tools and principles. It is filled with concepts, illustrations, activities, sample work sheets, and real life Laurie Stories, all of which demonstrate how to think the unthinkable, and make the impossible possible.

Each chapter of this book contains a Laurie Story. A Laurie Story is a story about me that illustrates when my rich choices paid off and when my poor habits prevented me from succeeding. It is my hope that, by including these personal accounts, you will be encouraged and motivated to learn from my past successes and failures.

My goal is to motivate you to eliminate self-defeating poor habits, and to inspire you to make intelligent and informed rich choices. My hope is that you will continually move in the direction of your dreams and goals. I have divided this book into two sections: Life Management and Financial Management.

LIFE MANAGEMENT

The Life Management section is designed to help you understand the impact your choices have on your future. Life Management techniques cover: setting personal goals, consistently doing your best, effectively managing your thoughts and your time, taking appropriate risks while eliminating your fears, maintaining healthy relationships, and designing your life with passion. Life Management skills are essential to living a healthy and prosperous life.

FINANCIAL MANAGEMENT

The Financial Management section is designed to help you become an optimistic, responsible, and financially healthy individual. It covers fundamental skills including: financial goal setting, successful budgeting, intelligent consumption, basic money saving techniques, general investment principles, protecting yourself from identity theft, and successful credit card and checking account management. Financial literacy is an essential life skill and critical to your overall success.

We live in a country of opportunity and abundance, yet many of us are filled with self-doubt, hopelessness, and limited thinking. We are often told: "You can't, you won't, and you're not." I hope this book will inspire you to always say: "I can, I will, and I am!" *Live for today, choose for tomorrow!*

LET'S GO, LIFE IS WAITING!

> *We must open the doors of opportunity. But we must also equip our people to walk through those doors.*
>
> — *Lyndon B. Johnson*

BOOK ONE

LIFE MANAGEMENT

RICH CHOICES
VS. POOR HABITS

You don't get to choose how you're going to die or when. You only get to choose how you're going to live.

— Joan Baez

Personal growth is a lifelong and, sometimes, difficult task. Many people believe that first-hand experience is the best teacher. Fortunately for me, I've never held this opinion, and I have avoided a lot of heartache, pain, and D-R-A-M-A because of my willingness to learn from others. Personal growth and development can be made a little easier for those willing to do this.

You are solely responsible for your life. You create it through your choices. The greatest gift you've been given is the power of choice. Why not choose to learn from those whom you respect, admire, and love? ***Make it a habit to choose wisely.***

CHOICE is the act of making a selection – choosing an option. Every situation you encounter comes down to making a choice, and your choices create your life. The greatest gift you've been given is the power of choice. ***Make it a habit to choose wisely.***

HABITS are patterns of behavior. These patterns result from continual repetition. A habit results from behaviors that are often done without conscious thought. A habit is an established nature of the mind or character. The greatest gift you've been given is the power of choice. ***Make it a habit to choose wisely.***

We are what we repeatedly do. Excellence, then, is not an act, but a habit.

— Aristotle

RICH BY CHOICE

You can make your dreams come true and live the rich life by continually making rich choices while eliminating or avoiding poor habits. I want you to live as "richly" as possible and achieve all your dreams. Rich by Choice means we continually make choices to enhance our lives. The word "rich" has many definitions, one of which is "very productive and therefore financially profitable." Living richly means you produce and maintain nurturing relationships, good health, laughter, peace of mind, serenity, excellence, creativity, and of course, wealth. Lots of wealth. Rich is a state of mind AND a way of life.

POOR BY HABIT

To be poor is to have a state of mind that is disabled. To be poor means we continually make poor choices that block our success. In Greek, the word poor means "non-productivity". Mentally poor people live a sad, dejected and miserable life. We either fall victim to our bad habits and let them determine our future, or we gather up the courage to eliminate them. Without eliminating poor, non-productive habits, it is very unlikely you will achieve riches and wealth.

Continually making *Rich Choices* while eliminating *Poor Habits* is the key to being:

- Rich Rather Than Poor
- Wealthy Rather Than Broke
- Happy Rather Than Sad
- Optimistic Rather than Pessimistic

Rich vs. Poor

Rich is the opposite of poor. You already knew that. But, did you know that rich has nothing to do with how much money you have? Rich and poor are alike in that they reflect your state of mind and your outlook. Rich thinking is positive and optimistic while poor thinking is negative and pessimistic. If your attitude is positive and you continually make rich choices, you're more likely to create happiness and financial wealth. If your attitude is negative and you continually engage in or fail to eliminate poor habits, you will create a sad, poor life and will most likely be broke.

It's been said that if all the money in this country were distributed evenly among the entire population, within a short period of time a majority of it would end up back in the hands of those who originally had it. Did you know that two out of three lottery winners end up losing all their money within five years? What happens? We can all name rap stars, singers, actors, or other celebrities who've made millions of dollars yet ended up with nothing. Why do so many people who acquire wealth (money) end up losing it all?

They lose it all because they were never rich. They simply had wealth (money), and no amount of money can make a poor person rich. They had the mentality of a poor person and so they managed their lives and their money accordingly. They were Poor by Habit, not Rich by Choice.

If your **ATTITUDE** is:
POSITIVE – *you are* **RICH**
NEGATIVE – *you are* **POOR**

Wealthy vs. Broke

Both wealthy and broke refer to the amount of money you have (or don't have). They are both a result of your outlook and your approach to life. Wealth is the amount of money you have, which can be acquired as a result of making positive, rich choices. Many of us say we want to be rich; however, what we really want is wealth. When you're wealthy, you can afford to acquire whatever you want, because your wallet is full.

We may all experience times during our lives when we're broke. Broke is a temporary state; poor is a way of life (negative thinking). Broke can be a result of poor financial management. When you are broke, you can not afford to acquire whatever you want, because your wallet is empty.

If your **WALLET** is:
FULL – you are **WEALTHY**
EMPTY – you are **BROKE**

"One day a father of a very wealthy family took his son on a trip to the country with the firm purpose of showing his son how poor people can be. They spent a couple of days and nights on the farm of what would be considered a very poor family. On their return from their trip, the father asked his son, "How was the trip?" "It was great, Dad." "Did you see how poor people can be?" the father asked. "Oh Yeah" said the son. "So what did you learn from the trip?" asked the father. The son answered, "I saw that we have one dog and they had four. We have a pool that reaches to the middle of our garden and they have a creek that has no end. We have imported lanterns in our garden and they have the stars at night. Our patio reaches to the front yard and they have the whole horizon. We have a small piece of land to live on and they have fields that go beyond our sight. We have servants who serve us, but they serve others. We buy our food, but they grow theirs. We have walls around our property to protect us; they have friends to protect them." With this the boy's father was speechless. Then his son added, "Thanks dad for showing me how poor we are."

— Author Unknown

Now, you understand that Rich and Poor are a state of mind and that Wealthy and Broke are how much money you have. As the above story illustrates, what seemed to be a poor family to the father turned out to be a rich family to the boy. The boy perceived that the "poor" family was happy and productive, while the "wealthy" father viewed the family as "poor". The father clearly did not understand the difference between rich and poor. The fact that the family did not have a lot of wealth did not mean they were poor. You do not have to be wealthy to be rich, as his son rightfully concluded. The boy instinctively understood the difference between Rich and Poor.

Rich people enjoy every moment of every day, regardless of the amount of money they have. There is a big difference between being rich and being wealthy, and having them both, for many of us, is the ultimate dream. Your entire future is under your charge. Don't leave anything to chance.

It's Choice, Not Chance That Determines YOUR Future

- Each morning when you wake up, you can choose to be in a good mood or you can choose to be in a bad mood. *Choose to be in a good mood.*

- When something bad happens, you can choose to be a victim or you can choose to learn from the experience. *Choose to learn from it.*

- When your friends are whining and complaining, you can choose to complain too, or you can encourage them to take action and improve the situation. *Choose to be encouraging and constructive.*

- Every time you fail, you can call yourself a loser and view the situation as hopeless, or you can learn what not to do the next time. *Choose to learn from the experience.*

- When someone around you is in a bad mood, you can choose to let them negatively affect your mood, or you can choose to remain in a good mood. *Choose to remain in a good mood and stay positive.*

Eliminate your Poor Habits and replace them with Rich Choices. *The greatest gift you possess is the power of choice. Choose wisely.*

YOU Make it Happen

Aristotle said: "We are what we repeatedly do." Sometimes we expect too much but do too little. Are you waiting for someone or something outside yourself to make your dreams a reality? If so, it doesn't work that way! No one is going to care more about your dreams and aspirations than you do. Why should they?

Make positive, life expanding rich choices. Eliminate poor habits of behavior. In a world full of choices, the ones that move you in the direction of your dreams are the rich choices you make!

Make it a habit to choose wisely.

Optimism is essential to achievement and it is also the foundation of courage and true progress.

— Lloyd Alexander

BREAK A HABIT BEFORE IT BREAKS YOU

Have you ever said to yourself, "I'll never do that again," only to do it again and again? We all have some poor habits that block our success and prevent us from doing our best. Habits provide us with a temporary fix, a way of release from frustration, a way to relax.

Bad habits can be broken. Eliminating negative personal habits and replacing them with good ones requires commitment and practice. To get to the bottom of why you do what you do, go back to basics. Ask yourself the Five W's: Who? What? When? Where? and Why?

☀ RICH CHOICES ☀

Break a Habit Before it Breaks You

- Who? With whom do you normally engage in bad habits?
- What? What do you get out of it?
- When? Is there a certain time of day or week when you fall into your habit?
- Where? Are there specific locations or activities that create a mood that tempts you to indulge in your habit?
- Why? Why do you do it?

Answering these questions will help you figure out why you do what you do. One of the greatest challenges in life is breaking a poor habit. Each of us has some poor habit we must challenge ourselves to eliminate. Poor habits prevent us from moving forward in life. Sometimes changing your habits requires changing your thinking. You see, your thinking creates all your ideas and your ideas lead to your actions. Your actions shape your habits, and of course – your habits make your life. If there's something in your life that's not working for you, change your thinking first, then challenge yourself to honestly reflect on what poor habits are blocking your success.

A LAURIE STORY

**In High School I Proved to Myself I Could Fail.
In College I Proved to Myself I Could Succeed.**

Life consists in what a man is thinking of all day.

— *Ralph Waldo Emerson*

Growing up in my family there was never any talk of going to college. The expectation was that all the kids would graduate from high school. This was considered the BIG accomplishment. I graduated and settled into a regular, boring, hourly job and lifestyle. I was working at a department store and was becoming quite happy with my "nine to five" way of life.

I felt like a real adult. I was working and making enough to survive. This was all I needed and wanted. I was able to buy my own clothes, keep my car on the road, and maintain an active social life. Back then, I thought that was enough. Yippie! No more school! Or so I thought…

A year after I graduated from high school my Mom suggested I do something more constructive with my life. For the very first time she said – "GO TO COLLEGE!" I graduated from high school with very poor grades. I had absolutely no intention of going to college. It had never occurred to me that I could go, given my poor academic performance.

I have eight sisters and brothers. I am number six. Up to this point in my life, my older brother, Kevin, was the only relative to go to college. This includes parent, grandparent, first cousin, or anyone else. To this day, I'm not really sure how I was accepted into college. My mother, however, was instrumental in giving me this opportunity. I may not know how I got in, but I'll never forget how I arrived on campus.

When it was time for me to leave home, we drove to upstate New York. Seven hours into our drive, we ran over a very large rock that punctured a hole in the gas tank. Since I didn't want to leave home, I perceived this as good news. I was relieved. Mother, on the other hand, had a different idea. We took public transportation back to Long Island, borrowed a vehicle, and began our trip all over again. I complained the entire way.

I was scared and felt like going to school was simply a waste of time. We completed the ten-hour trip and, when my mother was about to leave, I ran after the vehicle, pleading not to be left. With this, she stopped the car and said, "Look. All I ask is that you stay for one week. That way you cannot go through life saying you didn't have the opportunity to go to college." I was stunned. How dare she be philosophical while I was being dramatic? Up to that moment, I had never thought of school as an "opportunity."

During that first week, I decided to challenge my past academic performance. I made up my mind to stay for one semester and to answer these basic questions: "Could I get a decent grade if I tried?" "What would happen if I changed my inner dialog and started to think in more positive, optimistic ways?" "Was it possible I could develop better study habits and improve my academic performance?"

That week I engaged in serious and honest self-examination. I set goals and made a commitment to try harder. I was going to do my best, regardless of the amount of time and energy it required. I set out to determine the cause of my failing high school grades. I studied incessantly, and I was diligent. I was prepared for all my exams. I did not:

- Use cliff notes
- Cram at the last minute for an exam
- Copy other student's work
- Use cheat sheets
- Cut classes
- Assume I was going to fail

I was a new me! I took corrective action and I developed new habits. I became organized, focused, and determined. I was enthusiastic and I began to visualize my success. I implemented all the study habits I had learned earlier in school, but had never bothered to apply. I even used index cards. Teachers no longer ignored or disliked me. They no longer viewed me as a loser who was just taking up space in the classroom. They knew who I was, but this time it was for the right reasons. I had successfully eliminated many of my negative study habits.

I made the Dean's list with a 3.8 average. I was shocked. For the first time in my life, I received academic recognition. I was proud. More importantly, I learned I could achieve whatever I wanted, in school and in life. I just had to get honest with myself, take corrective action, and apply myself. Funny thing is… growing up, I remember adults telling me I could do anything if I would just apply myself. Obviously, I chose to ignore their suggestions.

My academic success forced me to face the bitter truth. During high school, I developed the habit of making excuses for my negative attitude and poor academic performance. I had convinced myself that I was academically challenged and that I couldn't do any better. All those years I spent looking for shortcuts could have been spent being a good student. In high school, I simply committed to maintaining everyone's poor impression of me. No wonder my high school teachers disliked me; I didn't do any work. To them, I was a loser, and I did nothing to change their opinion of me.

My life at home during high school was no picnic either. I wasn't trusted and my freedom was limited. Had I made the decision earlier to apply myself in school, my home life probably would have improved as a result. I finally understood that it took the same amount of energy for me to fail as it did for me to succeed. Once I made up my mind to change my study habits and to do better, I did better.

This early college experience taught me a lot about my thinking. In high school, I created my reality by complaining, whining, blaming, cheating, and being defensive. These negative habits only helped to diminish my greatness. My attitude was bad and my thoughts were self-defeating.

As simple as it sounds, my life improved once I changed my thinking and my attitude. My thinking created my ideas and my ideas created my actions. My actions produced my habits and my habits were producing my life. My habits accurately reflected the state of my life. By changing my thinking, my actions changed. Once I changed my actions, I gained more confidence as to who I was and what I could accomplish. Once I set a goal and visualized grades better than my usual 40's, 50's, and 60's, I outperformed even my own expectations.

How you see the world reflects your thinking. How you live your life reflects your habits. Your attitude determines your aptitude. If you're a student who's doing well in school, I applaud you, congratulations! If you're a student who thinks you could do a little better, begin by changing your

thinking and your attitude towards your academic life. Don't view school so negatively; don't hate it so much. End the cycle of feeling powerless, angry, and hopeless.

Remember, most of us have some poor habit that blocks our success. Regardless of what your poor habit is, force yourself to change your thinking, view things more positively, and work to replace your poor habit with a rich choice. Erase the pattern of thinking negatively and replace it with a pattern of thinking about what you can achieve and what you can be.

A man's mind may be likened to a garden, which may be intelligently cultivated or allowed to run wild; but whether cultivated or neglected, it must, and will, bring forth. If no useful seeds are put into it, then an abundance of useless weed seeds will fall therein, and will continue to produce their kind. Just as a gardener cultivates his plot, keeping it free from weeds, and growing the flowers and fruits which he requires, so may a man tend the garden of his mind, weeding out all the wrong, useless, and impure thoughts, and cultivating toward perfection the flowers and fruits of right, useful, and pure thoughts, By pursuing this process, a man sooner or later discovers that he is the master gardener of his soul, the director of his life. He also reveals, within himself, the laws of thought, and understands with ever-increasing accuracy, how the thought forces and mind elements operate in the shaping of his character, circumstances, and destiny.

— James Allen

Activity

We Are What We Repeatedly Do!

Do you have a poor habit which is preventing you from doing your best? Take some time to think about something you'd like to work on. Write it down. Here are some suggestions of poor habits:

- poor eating habits
- poor sleeping habits
- poor listening habits
- poor study habits
- poor time management
- poor thinking habits
- poor spending habits
- giving in to fear
- trying to succeed alone
- unwilling to help others
- vague goals or, worse yet, no goals at all
- pessimism, sarcasm, cynicism
- procrastination
- clutter, pack rat
- bad temper
- selfishness
- laziness
- gossiping
- jealousy
- lack of enthusiasm
- lack of commitment

The poor habit I'd like to eliminate is:

_____

To get to the bottom of why you do what you do, get back to basics and ask yourself the following questions: **Who? What? When? Where? Why?**

- With **Whom** do I normally engage in this poor habit? _____
- **What** do I get out of it? _____
- **When** do I do it? Is there a certain time of day, week, or month when I fall into this habit? _____
- **Where** does it normally occur? Are there specific locations or activities that create a mood that tempts me to indulge in my habit? Where? _____
- **Why** do I do it? Be honest! _____

What steps am I prepared to take to rid myself of this poor habit?

_____
_____
_____

And yet not choice but habit rules the unreflecting herd.

— William Wordsworth

PERSONAL GOAL SETTING

All successful people are big dreamers. They imagine what their
future could be, ideal in every respect, and then they work every day
toward their distant vision, that goal or purpose.

— *Brian Tracy*

Where are you now? Where do you want to be in the future? How do you get there? There are different types of goals, some may be financial, others more personal – like becoming a better student, athlete, or dancer, getting a promotion at work, transitioning into a new career, etc. Goal setting is the process of identifying what you want and when you want it. Goal setting provides direction to your life, gives you a way to measure your progress, and helps you focus your energy on important things.

Do you live each day with a worthy personal goal in mind? Can you vividly see yourself achieving your personal goal? Do you imagine what you'll feel like when you reach it? Your personal goals are a reflection of your needs, your wants, and your desires. Each of us will have a different set of personal goals. Take time to think about your specific goals and keep your mind on the payoff!

The secret to effective goal setting is in knowing where you are now, where you want to go in the future, and developing a plan to get there. Take the time to think about what you want, both short and long-term. Commit to your goals by first putting them in writing.

☀ RICH CHOICES ☀

Personal Goal Setting

The key to effective goal-setting is to make sure your personal goals are:
- Specific
- Realistic
- Flexible
- Measurable
- Meaningful

Specific

Vague goals produce vague results! Goals are specific things you want to accomplish within a certain period of time. When you set a goal make sure it is definite and precise. Hazy goals produce hazy results.

Realistic

Your goals must be realistic and reasonable; otherwise you may become frustrated and abandon your plans. Make sure your goal is attainable. For example, if one of your personal goals is to improve your physical health and well being, then it's realistic to commit to exercising and eating healthy. It's unrealistic to try to workout for three hours a day if you haven't exercised in a year. Start with 30 minutes per day, and then increase your time as you become more physically fit.

Flexible

Be practical; make your goals a part of your life, even if plans change. As things in your life change you may be required to make adjustments to your plans. Don't be so rigid that you have to start over with a whole new plan. Stay on track. If something comes up unexpectedly, deal with it and modify your plan to fit into your life. Be flexible and continue to work towards your goals.

Measurable

Set benchmarks or targets, so you can measure your progress. It's a great feeling to look back, track your progress, and see how well you've done. Keep in mind that reaching a long-term goal may depend on achieving several short-term goals along the way. This will allow you to measure your success more easily. Plan a small reward for each segment achieved, then a king-size reward for the big targets achieved.

Meaningful

Identifying meaningful goals is the key to staying motivated and to achieving them. You won't be committed to a goal if it's not important to you. Therefore, choose meaningful goals that are significant and worthy. Meaningful goals will give purpose to your life!

Do something every day to reach your goals. Keep a picture or a token with you to constantly remind you of your goals and to keep you focused. Don't get discouraged, don't make excuses, and don't quit. Hang in there. Setting goals gives you a purpose. Think about how great you're going to feel when you accomplish your goals. Visualize the benefits. Identify and commit to your worthy goals, and do what it takes to achieve them.

A LAURIE STORY

Inch by Inch It's a Cinch!

Sow a thought, and you reap an act;
Sow an action, and you reap a habit;
Sow a habit, and you reap a character;
Sow a character, and you reap a destiny.

— *Charles Reader*

New Years day is a time when many of us seriously consider what we could do to improve our lives. We make resolutions that unfortunately, we don't keep. A couple of years ago, I decided to set a goal. This time, however, I decided to set a more realistic goal, one I knew I could keep. In the past, I had given up on my goals too quickly. I gave up because they were too overwhelming and too broad.

The goal I set for myself was to read more. Weeks and months passed and I wasn't reading anything. This was one of my bad habits. Occasionally I would read a magazine, but I wanted to develop the habit of reading.

The first couple of weeks were actually very difficult. I would put off reading until the very end of the day. I wanted to forget about my commitment because it felt like work, but I stuck with it. As a result, I created a new habit.

I achieved my goal and developed my new habit by using the steps outlined in this chapter. My goal was:

- Specific – I wanted to develop the habit of reading.

- Realistic – I took little steps and committed to reading for just five minutes a day, everyday. This made it easy to stick to my plan, after all, who can't devote five minutes a day towards improving their life? This is what is meant by the phrase, "Yard by yard, it's hard, but inch by inch, it's a cinch."

- Flexible – Reaching my goal was easy because I could read at any time of the day and I could read whatever I wanted.

- Measurable – Five minutes eventually turned to 15 minutes, and 15 minutes turned to hours.

- Meaningful – It was important to me to improve myself in this way. It's easy to commit to something that's important and meaningful.

Today, I read a lot more and I enjoy it. Reading is no longer something I dread. I set a goal and developed the qualities I wanted for myself by using the steps outlined above. I successfully turned a bad habit into a good one. I visualized myself succeeding and I didn't give up. I became an avid reader.

> *You must take action now that will move you towards your goals. Develop a sense of urgency in your life.*
>
> *— Les Brown*

ACTIVITY

Step Into the Future!

List three of your personal goals. Putting your goals in writing will help you outline a plan for achieving them. Be precise and outline your specific strategy for how you are going to reach them. Unclear goals are useless and meaningless. In the second column write down what you need to do to make your goals a reality. Are you currently doing any of these things?

GOALS	ACTIONS
1. _____	_____
2. _____	_____
3. _____	_____

If you prepare yourself... you will be able to grasp opportunity for broader experience when it appears.

— *Eleanor Roosevelt*

"Tap In" to
Your Full Potential

Choose a job you love, and you will never have to work a day in your life.

— *Confucius*

Have you every wondered why... Some people say they're going to do something and don't do it? While others say they're going to do something and then do it?

The difference is that some people are only interested while others are fully committed. One of the key ingredients to achieving success in life is to fully and completely commit to a goal or dream. When you go from being just interested in something to being fully committed to it, you produce results. When you commit, you become unstoppable and you're willing to do whatever it takes to make your goals and dreams a reality.

☀ RICH CHOICES ☀

"TAP IN" To Your Full Potential

- Be Proactive
- Focus Your Energy
- Ignore Your Critics
- Ask For Constructive Feedback
- Go Beyond Interest, Get Committed
- Never Say "I Can't"

Be Proactive

A stitch in time saves nine is a proverb about being proactive. When we're proactive we do what needs to be done before we need to do it. For example: replacing old batteries or printer cartridges before necessary, fixing a leak before it gets worse, or replacing worn, balding car tires prior to having a blow-out. Think about it? Is there ever a good time to have a flat tire? No! Being proactive helps you avoid wasting valuable time, energy, and money on last minute fixes. John F. Kennedy put it best when he said, "The time to repair the roof is when the sun is shining."

FOCUS YOUR ENERGY

Picture, feel, and imagine yourself as a person who gets things done. Concentrate on the positive results your actions will provide. Our lives are very full and there are many activities that distract us from focusing on what's important. When asked what the first requisite for success is, Thomas Edison said: "It is the ability to apply your physical and mental energies to one problem incessantly without growing weary." Individuals who demonstrate an on-going commitment to keep trying until they achieve their goals are the real winners in life. Don't waste time on trivial, unimportant tasks that simply drain your time and resources. Identify and focus your energy on meaningful, productive activities.

IGNORE YOUR CRITICS

Many of us don't take chances in life because we fear what others will say, do, or think. Who cares what they think? Don't let the fear of criticism prevent you from achieving your goals. Don't let your own personal ambition be destroyed by critics. It's easy to watch and criticize from the sidelines. Critics don't have anything going on in their lives. If they did, they would be handling their own business. Become someone who makes things happen.

ASK FOR CONSTRUCTIVE FEEDBACK

When I worked in a corporate environment, I was responsible for hiring employees for my division. One particular interview really stood out. When the interview ended and we said our good-byes, the young college student left my office. He returned five minutes later. Peeking his head into my office he said, "uh, excuse me Ms. Johnson, how did I do?" I was pleasantly surprised and impressed by his inquiry. He wanted to know what he could do to improve his interviewing skills next time. I immediately hired him because he showed a genuine interest in improving his interviewing skills. He was willing to be vulnerable. He wanted constructive feedback, not praise. Learn from your actions by asking for feedback.

Go Beyond Interest, Get Committed

You need to know what brings you joy and what doesn't because then you'll know how to channel your energy. When you're really committed to something and you absolutely love it, you have to do it because it brings you joy. Commitment is necessary to achieving a goal; interest alone is not enough. When you commit to your goals you produce outstanding results. Commit to something you enjoy!

Never Say "I Can't"

We are all driven by a deep inner longing to fulfill our potential. You can succeed at any task you decide to take on. Don't limit yourself by saying what you can't do. Always say "Yes, I can," "I'll try," or "I think I can." Say anything other then "No, I can't." Your unique gifts are waiting to be discovered. Your potential is limitless. Develop the habit of saying "yes" to yourself and to your potential.

> *The greatest crime in the world is not developing your potential. When you do what you do best, you are helping not only yourself, but the world.*
>
> *— Roger Williams*

A LAURIE STORY

I'm Committed and I'm Unstoppable.

Dancing appears glamorous, easy, delightful. But the path to paradise of the achievement is not easier than any other. There is fatigue so great that the body cries, even in its sleep. There are times of complete frustration, there are daily small deaths.

— *Martha Graham*

I know first hand what it's like to fail publicly. I love performing on stage. My preference is to dance with groups. Group performances make me feel less vulnerable than dancing solo. Years ago, a disastrous solo performance left me in tears.

During one of my performances my dear friend, Belinda, watched from the audience. After observing me for about a minute she obviously couldn't take it any longer. She gave me the old 'hand slash across the throat' signal, suggesting I cut my losses and exit the stage. I still vividly remember the pain and frustration I felt as I cried all the way home that night. It was a horrible experience made worse by the fact that the audience consisted of (what seemed like) the entire tap dance community.

Back then I danced with no emotion, no attitude, and no fire. I knew my performances were bad and I was willing to endure the pain of failing again and again in order to succeed. Audience members and acquaintances told me my performances were "fine." "Fine" was not good enough; I knew I could do better. I began to videotape myself. This is when I realized just how bad I was. I started to ask for constructive feedback. My friends and family finally confessed that I had "nothing going on from the ankles up." Ouch! I was no longer receiving generic compliments. I was now getting the kind of feedback that would help me improve and succeed.

I kept telling myself that since I had already done my worse, I could only get better; I had nothing else to lose! I wanted to tap dance and I wanted to perform. I began to focus my energy on my performance skills and I developed a passionate determination to succeed. With this determination came a willingness to temporarily fail in order to learn what not to do next time. **This was the point at which I became fully committed.**

Today, I continue working on becoming a more dynamic performer. At the end of every performance I simply tell myself "Ok, I did it again and I'm a better performer now then I was five minutes ago." In other words, I'm getting better simply by having the guts to act with courage, ignore my critics, and to keep trying. I am willing to endure additional pain, embarrassment, and heartache if that's the price I have to pay to reach my goal. I am willing to keep trying and yes, in some instances, failing. I'm not sure I'll ever reach the point where I'm completely satisfied with my performance. In a way that's good... because I will continue to grow and to improve.

The fastest way to success is to double your failure rate.

— *Thomas Watson*

ANOTHER LAURIE STORY

What Do the Hula Hoop and Lotus 123 Have in Common?

What looks like a loss may be the very event which is subsequently responsible for helping to produce the major achievement of your life.

— *Srully D. Blotnick*

When I was about six years old my mother obviously thought I was very cute and talented. She would dress me in really fancy clothes and take me into New York City to audition for various television and print commercials. On most occasions, the auditions were easy and predictable. I usually knew what the commercial was for, so I had some idea what I would be expected to do. There was one occasion however, when I didn't know what the audition was for. It turned out to be a life changing event. I learned never to say "I can't."

It was a cold winter day in Manhattan. My mother drove me into "The City" from Long Island. We parked the car and walked several blocks to where the audition was being held. I was relieved when my mother finally announced she had found the building because I remember being very cold. I was especially cold because of the very short dress I was wearing.

This commercial audition was different from previous ones because there was no time to prepare. On previous occasions there had been a lobby, an elevator, or a waiting area for us to get ready or for my mother to remind me what to do. On this occasion, however, we located the address, opened the door and there we were. A man stood blocking the doorway. He looked at me and asked, "Can you hula hoop?"

Up to that point in my very short life I don't think I had really disappointed my mother the way I was about to. Without giving my response any thought, I quickly said "No, I can't." He looked up at my mother and said, "Sorry, we can't use her." There was no opportunity for us to respond, he quickly shut the door. We didn't even get to step inside the building. I was freezing.

My life changed during the long, cold walk back to the car and during the even longer drive back to Long Island. My mother preached, and yelled like never before. She lectured the entire way home and into the next day. Her bottom line: I should have said anything other then "No."

She explained to me that my responsibility in life was to seize opportunities and to always be willing to try something new. She didn't seem to care about the fact I knew I really couldn't hula hoop. She said that wasn't the point. Her point was: whenever I'm asked whether I can do something, the proper response is either yes, I'll try, I think so, or something similar.

My mother's nagging paid off fifteen years later during a job interview. The interviewer expressed his confidence in my ability to do the job. He said he had one final question. He asked: "Do you know Lotus 123?" Know it? I had never even heard of it! Of course, that's not what I said. I didn't have to think about my response. My mother's words of wisdom had become a way of life for me. I had learned a very valuable lesson that cold day in New York. Without giving any thought to my response, I enthusiastically replied, "Yes, I'm familiar with it!" I was offered the position.

That afternoon I discovered Lotus 123 was a spreadsheet software program and I quickly learned how to use it. The bottom line: don't count yourself out too soon. Don't limit yourself by saying what you can't do. Say yes to yourself and to your potential.

> *Every moment of one's existence one is growing into more or retreating into less.*
>
> *—Norman Mailer*

Activity

Commitment is Great!

What are you interested in?

_____

What are you committed to?

_____

Answering these two questions can help you figure out where to focus your energy and attention. Reflect back on a time when you went beyond just interest and really committed to a goal? Write down how you felt when you achieved it.

I committed to a goal when I:

_____

When I reached my goal I felt:

_____

You have what it takes. So go ahead, "TAP IN" To Your Full Potential and remember – that which you continue to do becomes easier. Find a worthy cause and commit to it. Commitment is great!

Failure is not an Option! List three things you're afraid to do. If you knew you couldn't fail, what actions would you take today to get started?

             Goals   Actions

1. _____   _____

2. _____   _____

3. _____   _____

> _I believe life is constantly testing us for our level of commitment, and life's greatest rewards are reserved for those who demonstrate a never-ending commitment to act until they achieve. This level of resolve can move mountains, but it must be constant and consistent. As simplistic as this may sound, it is still the common denominator separating those who live their dreams from those who live in regret._
>
> — _Anthony Robbins_

Always Do Your Best

Always do your best. What you plant now, you will harvest later.

— *Og Mandino*

A Plan to Live By

An elderly carpenter was ready to retire. He told his employer-contractor of his plans to leave the house-building business and live a more leisurely life with his wife enjoying his extended family. He would miss the paycheck, but he needed to retire. They could get by. The contractor was sorry to see his good worker go and asked if he could build just one more house as a personal favor. The carpenter said yes, but in time it was easy to see that his heart was not in his work. He resorted to shoddy workmanship and used inferior materials. It was an unfortunate way to end a dedicated career. When the carpenter finished his work the employer came to inspect the house. He handed the front-door key to the carpenter. "This is your house, " he said, "my gift to you." The carpenter was shocked! What a shame! If he had only known he was building his own house, he would have done it all so differently. So it is with us. We build our lives, a day at a time, often put-ting less than our best into the building. Then with a shock we realize we have to live in the house we have built. If we could do it over, we'd do it much differently. But we cannot go back. You are the carpenter. Each day you hammer a nail, place a board, or erect a wall. "Life is a do-it-yourself project," someone has said. Your attitudes and the choices you make today, build the "house" you live in tomorrow. Build wisely!

— *Author Unknown*

Have you thought about the impact your decisions today will have on the "house" you'll live in tomorrow? Your current attitudes and choices create your future. We are all carpenters of our own lives and we must construct a solid foundation during our early stages. It's more difficult to try to re-build your "house" years later when normal wear and tear has taken its toll and the structure begins to deteriorate. Always maintain a positive attitude and always do your best.

☀ RICH CHOICES ☀

Always Do Your Best

- Be Conscientious
- Always Follow Through
- Aspire To Greatness
- Persist Under Pressure
- Provide Results Not Reasons

BE CONSCIENTIOUS

Sloppy work is a reflection of the person who produced it. No one will respect you or your work if it's sloppy. *Just emagine if i sent a lettir of introduckion to you and I don't took a time to use spell checkker, what would you tink of me?* To be conscientious is to be meticulous, careful, particular, fastidious, reliable, and diligent. Taking pride in your work is one of the keys to achieving success in life. Be thorough, be conscientious!

ALWAYS FOLLOW THROUGH

If you say you're going to do something, then by all means, follow through and get it done. When you're unreliable, you'll end up feeling guilty and worthless. Commit and follow through.

ASPIRE TO GREATNESS

The higher your aspirations, the higher your achievements. There are no shortcuts in life, so don't waste your valuable time looking for any.

Success and achievement come from hard work, commitment, dedication and persistence. Aspire to greatness and commit to doing your best work.

PERSIST UNDER PRESSURE

To maximize your potential, it's critical that you remain focused during the difficult times. When the going gets tough, you must train your mind to go the extra mile. We are all driven by a deep inner desire to fulfill our potential. However, most of our potential is unused because many of us are getting by on just a small percentage of our mental and physical capacities. Be confident and be willing to do just a little bit more, even if you're tired. Everyday you put off doing something makes it more difficult later on. Always do a little more than you think you can. Persist under pressure!

PROVIDE RESULTS, NOT REASONS

Accepting responsibility for your actions is the hallmark of good character. No one gets through life without their share of problems, mistakes, and setbacks. Setbacks are opportunities to make improvements, not excuses. It's easy to find fault in others and to look outside ourselves for solutions. Learn from your mistakes and failures. Effective and productive people discipline themselves and they never rely on excuses. Focus on your critical objectives, strive to deliver results. No Excuses, ever!

Every day we make choices that affect the rest of our lives. Whether you're entering junior high school, heading off to college, or counting down the days to your 21st birthday, strive to live a life in which you realize your full value and purpose. Avoid making decisions you may regret later in life. Take pride in whatever you do, maintain a positive attitude, and always strive to do your best.

Developing the habit of doing your best will help you to become productive and to gain more in life. When you enjoy what you're doing, it's easy to do your best. Consider what happens to individuals who go to work everyday at a job they dislike. They don't do their best because the only reason they go to work is for the money. They feel trapped and end up living a life they loathe. This is how it was for me when I worked at a corporate job. I was miserable, empty, unful-filled, and unmotivated.

There are no perks without the work! Be willing to do what it takes to get what you want. When your thoughts and actions are consistently focused on doing your best, you are more self-disciplined and less likely to be unproductive. In life there are no perks without the work. You can't have:

- JOY without RESPONSIBILITY
- APPROVAL without ACCOUNTABILITY
- PLEASURE without DEDICATION
- GRATIFICATION without COMMITMENT
- FRIENDSHIP without LOYALTY
- SUCCESS without SACRIFICE
- LOVE without A JOYFUL HEART

> *It's a funny thing about life; if you refuse to accept anything but the best, you very often get it.*
>
> — *Somerset Maugham*

A LAURIE STORY

Measure Twice, Cut Once!

> *If I had eight hours to chop down a tree, I would spend six sharpening my axe.*
>
> — *Abraham Lincoln*

When I was a teenager my mother taught me how to sew. On one occasion (during which I was unsupervised) I was too lazy to place the cutting board on the bed prior to cutting the pattern. I was in a hurry. I simply placed the fabric on the bed, laid the pattern on top of the fabric, and began to pin and cut. Imagine the trouble I was in when my mom realized her quilt had been cut into a pair of pants. *Oooops!*

On another occasion I was trying to be helpful when I poured transmission fluid into the oil tank of our family car. The containers looked the same and I obviously didn't bother to read the label or to ask questions. But it didn't stop there. I washed our next family car with the wrong solvent and removed its shiny, new finish. Clearly I was not being conscientious, nor did I learn from my previous experiences.

One day, my sister made the mistake of asking me to perm her hair. I lied when I told her I had read the instructions indicating the product should be left on for only 20 minutes. I realized I was in trouble when, after an hour, my sister began to complain of a burning and tingling sensation. She looked very odd during the next couple of weeks when her hair slowly began to fall out and the bald spots surfaced.

When I was in college I had a lot of holes in the walls of my apartment. These holes resulted from my attempts to hang pictures without taking the time to measure and to find the wall studs first. I also loved to redecorate and to paint. The problem was I just started painting without taking the necessary precautions. I didn't lay drop cloths, I didn't have rags readily available, and I didn't use tape to indicate where the colors should not touch. I just started painting. I always knew it would be a big, huge mess in the end - and it always was. I spent hours re-painting, touching up, and cleaning up what should have taken only ten minutes.

These situations (and others) could have been avoided if I had read the instructions, asked for help, performed additional preparation, or verified my steps prior to taking action. Clearly, these are instances when I was not doing my best. Additionally, I made matters worse when I gave excuses for my actions instead of owning up to, and learning from my mistakes. Sometimes doing our best is as simple as measuring twice and cutting once.

> *Winning is not a some-time thing; it's an all-the-time thing. You don't do things right once in a while; you do them right all the time. Winning is a habit.*
>
> — *Vince Lombardi*

Activity

Is That Your Best Work?

Are you happy with the direction in which your life is headed? Can you recall an instance in which you were disappointed with yourself because you did not do your best work? Write down an occasion in which you did not do your best. What happened? If presented with the opportunity to do it again, what would you do differently?

_____

_____

_____

_____

_____

_____

_____

_____

_____

_____

_____

_____

_____

_____

We are all in the gutter, but some of us are looking at the stars.

— Oscar Wilde

It's Your Body – Protect It, Respect It

If any thing is sacred, the human body is sacred.

— *Walt Whitman*

My motivation for writing this book came one day in 2002 when I saw a preview for a movie about to be released. The plot of the movie left me shocked, disturbed, and disgusted. The movie was based on a religious concept and its plot challenged the main character, a very young man, to take a vow of celibacy during the 40 days of Lent. This film and others like it negatively impact young people and our society. Up to this point in my life, I never thought about writing a book.

This chapter, more than any other, addresses my primary area of concern for young people. I've said it before and I'll say it again: the choices you make today shape your future. Some of your actions, once taken, cannot be undone.

There is a lot of self-destruction going on among young people. For the past several years I've been on the road and have spent a lot of time with young adults. I see an alarming number of young people drinking excessively, spending money frivolously, and engaging in other questionable activities. What is causing this tidal wave of aggressive self destruction?

Declining values and morality are impacting our culture. Without moral absolutes – what's left? If we all just do what is fashionable and what "feels good," we're heading for trouble. If morality depends on the particular situation, we will ultimately lose our integrity and self-respect. This will result in personal hopelessness and social chaos.

When it comes to your physical well being, you must make rich choices.

☀ RICH CHOICES ☀

It's Your Body – Protect It, Respect It

- Avoid the Quick Fix
- Practice Self Control
- Think Twice Before Getting Physical
- Ask For Help
- Appreciate Your Uniqueness
- Empower Yourself By Improving Your Self Esteem
- Eat Smart, Stay Fit
- Beer Responsible
- Think Before You Ink
- Don't Try To Hurt A Parent By Engaging In Self Destructive Activities
- Diffuse Peer Pressure

AVOID THE QUICK FIX

We live in a country where we're always looking for quick fixes. Advertisers use subtle and clever techniques to convince us that we need immediate gratification in all areas of our lives. We're constantly bombarded with the message that there's an easy solution to every problem and that it's good to find quick and easy ways to feel good!

- Had too many drinks? Take an aspirin for the hangover.

- Can't sleep? Take a sleeping pill.

- Having difficulty waking up? Grab a shot of caffeine.

- Need to lose weight? Consider gastric bypass surgery.

- Not getting enough calcium in your diet? Take a calcium supplement.

- Afraid you might have a wreck while driving drunk? Get a designated driver.

- Lacking self esteem because you think your nose is out of proportion? Hire a plastic surgeon.

Not one of these solutions addresses the real problem. They represent quick fixes to deeper issues. Before you develop habits that are detrimental to your physical or emotional well being, take some time to think about the cause of the problem and address it directly. If, for instance, you're having trouble sleeping, then figure out why you can't sleep. Perhaps you're under too much stress, or maybe it has something to do with your diet. Addressing symptoms and ignoring deeper issues can lead to addiction and other self destructive behaviors. Look for solutions that address the cause of the problem. Don't put band aids on issues that need greater attention.

Practice Self Control

Chances are you've heard the following three expressions: "Better safe than sorry," "Err on the side of caution," and "An ounce of prevention is worth a pound of cure." Exercising caution and self control before entering into a bad situation is better than having to make repairs and apologies later on. Ask yourself these questions: "What's the worse that can happen?" "How will this choice affect my future?" "Am I willing to live with that?" Practice self control, after all, prevention is better than a remedy. Your mind is the only thing over which you have complete control.

Think Twice Before Getting Physical

At some point in our lives we have all faced complicated and important choices. One such choice is whether or not to have sex. Before you become physically involved in a relationship, ask yourself the following very important questions:

- Why am I choosing this behavior?
- What are my limits?
- What values was I taught growing up?
- How important are these values to me now?
- Am I compromising my values and standards?
- What are my goals now?

- Will this action help me reach them?

- What are my long-term goals?

- Am I ready for this?

If any one of these questions makes you stop and think then do just that – stop and think. If you have trouble answering any one of these questions, talk with a friend or someone you trust. I recommend abstinence for every young person. It's never too late to try something new or to change your behavior. Abstinence is a choice you can make at any time. It's never too late.

Oftentimes we want to say "no" but because we want to look cool, or lack assertiveness, we don't know how. To be true to yourself you must assert yourself when the time comes to say no. Saying "NO" may not be easy, but if you don't say it for yourself, who will? Just Say "NO" or ...

- "Sorry, I can't right now."

- "I'm not ready to do that yet."

- "I don't feel like it."

- "Maybe later, thanks anyway."

- "I'm not like everybody else."

- "I have a headache." (This old standby has been working for centuries.)

If you don't respect yourself, no one else will. We may all experience awkward or uncomfortable situations related to sex, drugs, drinking, smoking, etc. How you handle it reflects your inner values and your sense of self worth. There are some choices that don't have as profound an impact on our lives as others. When it comes to these critical issues, choose wisely! Nothing endures more than respect for oneself.

Ask For Help

We all need help at various times in our lives. If you're in a relationship that you feel is moving in a direction which makes you uncomfortable, ask for help. Your love life shouldn't be so all encompassing that you can't get your work done, hang out with friends, or break up without fear of being harmed. Controlling behavior in any relationship is not love, it's abuse. Seek insight from a parent, an adult relative, a school counselor, a co-worker, or someone else you trust. If you're not getting the support you need at home than get it elsewhere. Getting someone else's point of view may be just what you need to help you deal with a stressful situation. Talking with someone can help you sort out what actions to take and which not to take.

APPRECIATE YOUR UNIQUENESS

I travel around the country. During my travels I listen to, interact with, and observe young people. I see how vulnerable they are to the dominant cultural messages perpetuated by the media. Overly aggressive advertisers target young people because they are a fast-growing segment of society and because they have money to spend. Additionally, young people are new consumers. Advertisers take advantage of their inexperience.

There's a never-ending pressure on us to become the perfect commodity. This is especially true of girls and women. We are constantly bombarded with the message that what's important is our clothing, our fragrance, our swimsuit, our bodies, our make-up, our hair, our teeth, and our looks. Girls and women are more vulnerable to these pressures to consume and conform because our bodies are viewed as objects just about everywhere we look. We're preoccupied with our looks and we're willing to go to great lengths to meet the criteria set forth in movies, radio ads, magazines, song lyrics, billboards, commercials, ads, etc. We're all subjected to unrealistic beauty standards.

Instead of focusing on unrealistic goals, focus on what makes you unique and on creating a healthier, happier life. Remember – we each excel at different things and our talents are constantly developing. Think about what you're good at and what you enjoy, and build on these talents. Take pride in your unique skills and in the talents you have or want to develop. Accept and appreciate your uniqueness.

EMPOWER YOURSELF BY IMPROVING YOUR SELF-ESTEEM

Self-esteem is how much you value and take pride in yourself. It's your opinion of your accomplishments, skills, qualities, and character. Self-esteem is how you feel about yourself after you've compared yourself with what you want to be, with how you view what you are.

While growing up, I went to eleven different schools. NO! My family never moved. Switching schools so frequently was very difficult. I was always the new kid who was ignored, beat-up, disliked, or teased. Rather than focus on what was bad about always being the new kid at school, let me tell you what I learned.

Being the one on the outside looking in had its advantages. I observed that a lot of people don't think for themselves. They want the approval of others so desperately that they'll sacrifice their values to get it. I saw that people don't trust or believe in themselves. They need validation from others to feel good.

We all experience times in our lives when we feel unworthy or insecure. However, constant self-criticism diminishes your self-esteem further. The inner critic can be retrained. Positive self-talk is one of the primary ways to improve the way you feel about yourself. Accept what you can change and what you can't change.

When you're feeling like someone else has really "got it going on" and that the "grass is greener on the other side," take a few moments and water your own grass. Spend time focusing on your strengths. Pay attention to the compliments you receive. Play up what you do well. If you don't believe you're worthwhile, trust me when I tell you – no one else will believe it!

EAT SMART, STAY FIT

Proper exercise, diet, and nutrition are the foundation of a healthy lifestyle. Unfortunately, there are millions of Americans who don't eat and exercise properly. If you eat junk food, spend hours playing video games, believe that operating the television remote and walking from the sofa to the refrigerator is exercise, you need to think again. Look at yourself and ask the question: Are you happy with the way you look and feel? It's not just older and obese people who have issues. If you don't take proper care of your body now, you will pay for it later. So get off the sofa, start drinking water, do some sit-ups, and take the dog for a long walk.

BEER RESPONSIBLE

Young people today are drinking more heavily than ever before. They are also suffering the horrible consequences. This is especially true for girls and women. Females are less able to digest alcohol. Alcohol gets into our bloodstream faster, causing us to get drunker faster. Because we get drunk faster, we become addicted more quickly, and develop alcohol related diseases sooner than our male counterparts. Additionally, females who drink heavily are more likely to be victims of rape and sexual assault and to have unwanted pregnancies. Using drugs or alcohol can create situations that put you at risk. Minimize your risk by choosing responsible actions.

THINK BEFORE YOU INK

Tattoos are the latest fashion craze, they're everywhere. Not long ago they were associated with heavy-metal rockers, bikers, criminals, and social outcasts. But today it's no big deal; it's considered high-fashion and glamorous. When you're 16 years old, getting a tattoo seems like a terrific idea. When you're 20, you still think it's a good idea. But what about when you become an adult and your attitudes, values, career, friends, and life all change? What seemed like a brilliant idea just a few years ago is now making you feel self-conscious, and look foolish.

Tattoos are for life. Sure, they can be covered up or even removed, but removal is expensive, painful, and time consuming. According to the American Society of Dermatological surgery, over 50% of everyone receiving a tattoo wants it removed. Laser tattoo removal is one of the fastest growing areas of the dermatology industry. On average, it takes approximately 10 to 15 laser surgery sessions to remove a tattoo and costs around $400 – $800 per session. Even with all this treatment, the tattoo is still visible.

Are you absolutely certain of a design you want to wear on your body for the rest of your life? Consider the fact that so many people change their minds. Think carefully about whether you want to lock yourself into a fashion statement that might cause you aggravation and heartache later in life. Don't rush out and make a hasty decision. My advice to all of you considering a tattoo? Give it some more thought!

DON'T TRY TO HURT A PARENT BY ENGAGING IN SELF DESTRUCTIVE ACTIVITIES

Some of us don't have parents who provide guidelines and set limits. Some parents are involved in their own careers, love lives, and selfish social agendas. These parents deprive their children of the attention they need and deserve. Sometimes, because we're angry, we try to get back at a parent by getting into trouble. This is our way of getting the attention we so desperately want. Don't ruin yourself and your future by engaging in self destructive activities to gain the attention of a parent. You can't control the actions of anyone but yourself. Focus on what you do have and on what's good in your life. This may be difficult, but it's necessary. To do otherwise is to deny reality.

DIFFUSE PEER PRESSURE

Why is it that when I'm out socially with a group, there are always a few individuals who don't feel comfortable unless everybody's drinking? Sometimes, this can be annoying. I've been called a lot of things because of my unwillingness to succumb to peer pressure. The more pressure I receive to do something I don't want to do, the stronger I become. Peer pressure makes me feel like the instigators or troublemakers are saying, "Hey, you're just like us so do what we do." I'm not like everyone else and I don't want to be. Their pleading makes me more determined not to join in. I start to enjoy watching the instigators become frustrated as they beg, plead, or tease more.

If you find yourself sacrificing your self worth by doing what you don't want to do in order to be accepted, the price is too high.

WALK AWAY. Walk away because in the end you'll be held to a higher standard than those set by your acquaintances. Walk away and stay away.

To love oneself is the beginning of a lifelong romance.

— *Oscar Wilde*

A LAURIE STORY

The Writing's on the Wall!

We first make our habits, and then our habits make us.

—*John Dryden*

I've always enjoyed reading quotes and poems. While in high school I came across a verse from the Rubaiyat of Omar Khayyam which had a profound and lasting effect on me. The Rubaiyat is a collection of poems and the verse I'm talking about is from the section, "Being and Nothingness." It reads like this:

> *The moving finger writes; and having writ,*
> *Moves on; nor all your piety nor wit*
> *Shall lure it back to cancel half a line,*
> *Nor all your tears wash out a word of it.*

I can say, without hesitation, that this verse changed the course of my life. I memorized it and used it to continually remind myself that some actions, once taken, could not be undone or fixed. I viewed my life as a blank slate, chalkboard, or journal. My choices were filling the pages of my journal and all my actions, good and bad, were being recorded.

The "moving finger" symbolized my free-will and my choices. The definition of piety is goodness, faithfulness, godliness, and devoutness. Once the writing is on the wall, that's it. Nothing could erase it.

I've been in many situations in which I felt tempted, pressured, lured, interested, confused, fascinated, attracted, excited, willing, able, and scared – all at the same time. Let's face it, sometimes we just don't know what to do. In some instances, we don't have a lot of time to consider our options, make a decision, and then stand by that decision.

Whenever I'm scared, have doubts, or think my decision will get me into trouble or hurt my future; I recall this verse and say it to myself. It reminds me to THINK ABOUT MY OPTIONS AND CONSIDER THE CONSEQUENCES – before I take action. The thought of doing something that could ruin my future scares me enough to avoid taking stupid risks.

Napoleon Bonaparte wrote, "The best cure for the body is a quiet mind." Take some time to think through your choices. Assess the damage ahead of time by considering the worse case scenario. Before the occasion arises, practice what you would say if someone pressures you to do something you don't want to do. Stand tall, speak clearly and confidently. Life is a series of choices; err on the side of caution and reason. Don't go down the path of destruction by doing things which will hurt you or your future. Before making any major decisions, especially ones that can't be reversed, quiet your mind, think, and then choose wisely.

> *All that you want to be, you already are. All you have to do is move your awareness to that place and recognize the reality of your own soul.*
>
> *—John Rogers*

Activity

Your Future is Self-Determined!

Put the number in the blank that best tells your feelings.
4 – All the time
3 – Most of the Time
2 – Once in a while
1 – Hardly ever

_____ I am willing to do what someone else wants
_____ I speak up for myself
_____ I'm willing to say "No," even if it means hurting someone else's feelings
_____ When I say "No," I stick to my decision
_____ I keep my commitments to others
_____ I keep my commitments to myself
_____ I respect myself
_____ I make good decisions
_____ I turn down drugs and alcohol
_____ I think about my decisions prior to making them
_____ I do things I don't want to do because my friends convince me
_____ I compromise my values to be accepted by my peers
_____ I spend time with individuals even though I know they're not my friends and don't care about me
_____ I act impulsively

Review your responses.
• Are you pleased with your results? _____
• Are there some areas you need to improve? _____
• What are you going to do to about it? _____

> *Better by far you should forget and smile than that you should remember and be sad.*
>
> — *Christina Georgina Rossetti*

51

Your Thinking Creates Your Reality

Your thinking creates ideas:
Ideas lead to actions;
Actions shape your habits; and
Habits make your life.
If you don't like your life, change your thinking!

— *Laurie Johnson*

Your thinking creates your life because your thinking drives your choices and creates your habits. Your attitude about yourself stems from childhood experiences, parents, family, friends, and of course, your thinking.

Your inner conversations maintain your attitude. When you talk to yourself, is your dialog mostly positive or negative? Our ideas and values stem from our thoughts. The primary thing that separates us from other individuals is our thinking. Some of us find joy in a situation while others may find it dull and boring. Some of us make things happen while others simply watch, complain, and criticize.

If you're in need of an attitude

adjustment, alter your inner dialog. You can have anything you want simply by using the power of your mind. Thinking positively can help you:

- Reduce Stress and Worry
- Create Meaningful Relationships
- Boost Your Self Confidence
- Eliminate Negative Feelings
- Establish Inner Peace
- Take Charge of Your Life

☀ **RICH CHOICES** ☀

Your Thinking Creates Your Reality

- Focus On Today, Forget About Yesterday
- Commit To Something You Care About
- Be Enthusiastic
- View Setbacks As Opportunities
- Visualize Success
- Read Positive, Uplifting Materials

FOCUS ON TODAY, FORGET ABOUT YESTERDAY

Letting go of the past allows you to focus your energy on what's important and what's happening today. Let go of whatever happened yesterday, it's done with. You can't relive it and you can't change it. You can't change the past but you can create the future. Focus on future possibilities and enjoying every minute of today.

COMMIT TO SOMETHING YOU CARE ABOUT

It's easy to be upbeat when you're doing something you love. When you're engaged in an activity that brings you joy you are naturally motivated to do it and to do it well. Continually feed your mind, heart, and soul by committing to activities you care about.

BE ENTHUSIASTIC

The belief that your attitude determines your life experience works both ways. If you expect the worse, or continually reference your bad luck, you set yourself up for a life of limitations and setbacks. If you refer to yourself as a "stupid loser," that's what you will be. It's a self fulfilling prophecy. We become what we think we are.

Thinking positively and maintaining a positive attitude is a habit anyone can develop. Changing your thinking is the first step towards changing your life. When you think positively, you make the most powerful laws of life work in your favor. When you practice maintaining a positive attitude by eliminating negative thoughts, you permanently improve your consciousness. Everything that is great and magnificent becomes possible for you. Focus on what's good and on what is working well for you. As a man thinketh, so is he. Be enthusiastic about life!

VIEW SETBACKS AS OPPORTUNITIES

The potential for setbacks exists in every risk. Learn to view them as temporary detours. Remember, failure is your opportunity to learn what not to do next time. Success comes to those who believe there is always a way to overcome obstacles and challenges. Turning setbacks into opportunities is a strength successful individuals always practice. Analyze your mistakes and respond to setbacks like a winner. You can overcome any challenge!

VISUALIZE SUCCESS

Visualize what you want for yourself in the future. Tiger Woods was just a kid when he used an index card to write down that he would break the records established by many of the professional golfers he grew up watching and admiring. He believed it, visualized it, and he did it. Before Mark Spitz won 10 Olympic gold medals, he took pictures of himself wearing 10 gold medals. He made it happen. One of my many goals is to sit and chat with Oprah Winfrey on her daytime talk show. I've visualized it and I have already selected my outfit. I know it will happen.

READ POSITIVE, UPLIFTING MATERIALS

Eliminate thoughts, habits, and people that are keeping you from reaching your goals. Do whatever it takes to achieve this. Try reading for fifteen minutes a day from a positive, motivational book. Consistently reading positive materials will boost your self-belief and will help you continue to think positively. I recommend reading *The Greatest Salesman in the World* by Og Mandino. Of all the books I've read, this one single-handedly does it all. It's amazing!

> *The greater part of happiness or misery depends on our disposition, not our circumstances.*
>
> — *Martha Washington*

A LAURIE STORY

A Bad Attitude or a Bad Day?

Optimism is essential to achievement and it is also the foundation of courage and true progress.

— *Lloyd Alexander*

When I was in junior high school, I was unaware of my greatness. When asked anything about my life my reply was usually "I don't know" or "I don't care." I was disinterested in myself and in my future.

"I can't win, I'm a loser, that's just my luck, and I was never good at anything." This was my internal dialog. It became a way of life and a self-fulfilling prophecy. My negative outlook manifested itself in just about every area of my life, including my school work.

Whenever I had a reading comprehension assignment, I would look for shortcuts. Instead of reading a chapter in its entirety, I would waste time searching each page looking for key words I *hoped* would answer the questions. I spent hours completing a homework assignment that should have taken me 45 minutes to complete. My family and teachers explained to me how self-defeating this behavior was but sadly, I continued to do it my way, despite the very poor results.

There was a part of me that knew my shortcuts weren't working, yet I continued to take the longer, more difficult route. At the time it seemed easier, but in reality, I was wasting energy and getting nowhere. I knew I was capable of doing the work because whenever an adult sat with me and we read a chapter together, I quickly and accurately answered the questions.

I look back on this early academic experience and I ask myself: "Why did I look for shortcuts?" Why did I avoid reading the chapter first?" "Why didn't I do what I knew would get me better results?" Perhaps I was just lazy. Other reasons may have been a lack of:

- Motivation
- Interest
- Reward or Recognition
- Proper Guidance
- Focus, Concentration

- Meaningful Consequences
- Determination
- Enthusiasm
- Effort
- Support from Family, Teachers

I realize now that I was simply lazy. My laziness and self-defeating actions were fueled by my negative inner dialog. My laziness caused me stress because I spent so much time and energy avoiding activities I regarded as unpleasant, boring, difficult, or intimidating. My thinking was creating my reality.

Changing my inner dialog would have been the first step towards improving my life and changing my results. Unfortunately, I did not make any changes until a few years later. The Laurie Story in the chapter entitled, "Break a Habit Before it Breaks You" reveals how I finally changed my ways.

The dictionary is the only place success comes before work.

— *Vince Lombardi*

Activity

What Do Your Thoughts Say About You?

Are you a positive thinker? The true test of a positive thinker is someone who can be upbeat and optimistic during good and bad times. Your attitude is a major factor in determining your success in life.

Over the next couple of days, keep a journal of events in your life. Write down instances when you choose to be positive and optimistic rather than negative and pessimistic. After a couple of days read what you've written.

- Are you happy with your results?
- Do you see areas where you could have done better?
- Are there instances when you overreacted or responded poorly?

If so, jot down three ways you could have been more upbeat and optimistic in that situation. Are you willing to do these things?

Times when I was Pessimistic   Action to Take

1. _____   _____

2. _____   _____

3. _____   _____

> *To be nobody but yourself in a world which is doing its best,*
> *night and day, to make you everybody else means to fight the*
> *hardest battle which any human being can fight; and never*
> *stop fighting.*
>
> — *e.e. cummings*

THE CLOCK IS TICKING –
INTELLIGENT TIME
MANAGEMENT

Let him who would enjoy a good future waste none of his present.

— *Roger Ward Babson*

Time management is a learned life skill. Time management is controlling the sequence of events in your day-to-day life. We all have free will and we all possess the ability to choose which activities are important and which are not.

Making intelligent time management decisions is what determines our success at school, at work, and in life. Many of us are familiar with the expression: "Work smarter not harder." Let's take it a step further: "Work smarter on the right things."

It's easy to place value on tangible items like a car, an electronic game, or a house. When it comes to placing value on something intangible, like time, it's more difficult. Nevertheless, remember this: all your time is valuable.

Effective and productive people discipline themselves to do the tough stuff, regardless of how much they dislike it. They accomplish more than the average person and are much happier as a result. Sometimes the most difficult part of a task is getting started. Many of us procrastinate while others simply lack clear direction. The payoff and rewards for completing important tasks efficiently is often the difference between:

- Productivity and Boredom

- Accomplishment and Anxiety

- Success and Failure

☀ **RICH CHOICES** ☀

The Clock is Ticking – Intelligent Time Management

- You Don't "FIND" Time, You "MAKE" Time
- Develop a Plan, Not an Excuse
- Do the Unpleasant Thing First
- Save Time by Finishing What You Start
- Apply the 80/20 Rule
- Get Started

YOU DON'T "FIND" TIME, YOU "MAKE" TIME

My initial attempts at writing this book failed. I had to change my approach and find a way to get motivated. One of the few things that is fair about life is the fact that we all have 24 hours in a day. Some manage it efficiently while others squander it away. Remember, when you waste time, you waste yourself. Discipline yourself to use your time wisely. To make the most of your life, make the most of your time.

DEVELOP A PLAN, NOT AN EXCUSE

If You Fail to Plan, You Plan to Fail! Set a goal, develop a plan, put it in writing, and then take action. If something doesn't work out exactly as you had expected, take responsibly for it and get back on track. Relying on and believing your own excuses is a bad habit. Eventually your excuses create your reality and before long, you're accepting unfavorable circumstances as "just the way things are." You can have whatever you want in life the moment you stop making excuses, and giving your power away. A good plan is just the beginning. To get the results you want, plan your work to the very end and take into account all the possible obstacles that may develop. Plan your work and then work your plan.

Do the Unpleasant Thing First

Procrastination is the avoidance of doing something which needs to be done. We do this in part because we are attempting to avoid pain. Procrastinating results in feelings of guilt, worthlessness, self-doubt, and loathing. It can negatively impact our personal and financial lives. When you sit down to do your homework or some other project – do you do the easy stuff first? Do you procrastinate on activities you regard as unpleasant, boring, intimidating, or difficult? The greatest stress we experience comes from the amount of time and energy we spend avoiding something unpleasant. Get on with the task at hand and don't waste time dreading an activity, *get it over with!* Once it's behind you, you can move on to more enjoyable projects.

Save Time by Finishing What You Start

If you want to save time, make it a point to finish something while you're already working on it. Your commitment and resolve must be ongoing and consistent. If you're working on a really large project, consider breaking it into smaller, more manageable, sub-projects that can be completed in one sitting. You'll be less likely to become overwhelmed and to give up on the entire project. When you put off completing a project or sub-project, each time you begin again, you'll spend more time and energy trying to remember where you left off. The next time you find yourself saying, "I'll finish this tomorrow," keep working and force yourself to finish what you started. If a project or task can be completed in one sitting, go ahead and finish it. Save time by finishing what you start.

APPLY THE 80/20 RULE

The 80/20 Rule, or the *Pareto Principle,* is one of the most helpful concepts for managing your time and your life. It is named after its founder, the Italian economist and gardener, Vilfredo Federico Damaso Pareto. He first wrote about this concept in the late 1800's. Regarding money and influence, Pareto noticed that people divided naturally into what he called "the vital few" (the top 20 percent) and the "trivial many" (the bottom 80 percent).

He came about this discovery when he observed that 80 percent of the land in Italy was owned by 20 percent of the population. Later, while gardening, he observed that 80 percent of his peas were produced by 20 percent of the peapods.

When applied to your daily life, the 80/20 Rule states that 20 percent of your activities will account for 80 percent of your results. This means if you have a "to do" list of ten items, two of those items will turn out to be worth as much or more than the other eight items put together. The bottom line is this: of all the things you do during a day, only about 20 percent are really of any value and those 20 percent produce 80 percent of your results. Given this – it makes good sense to spend your time on the things that are of value.

Use of the 80/20 Rule can prove to be just the motivation you need to stop procrastinating, to become productive, and to focus on critical objectives.

The following scenario illustrates how the 80/20 Rule applies to a school fund raising activity:

All the students in your school are involved in a fund-raising effort. You are responsible for organizing and managing the activities. Some of your responsibilities include:

• Developing a Website

• Supervising Students in their Sales Activities

• Managing the Inventory

• Tracking Product Sales

• Coordinating Meetings

• Organizing Sales Activities

At the completion of the fund raising drive, here's how things will work out, on average:

- 80 % of sales will come from 20 % of the students

- 80% of revenues will come from 20% of the products

- 80 % of visitors to your website will see only 20 % of your web pages

- 20 % of your products will take up 80 % of your storage space

- 20 % of your meeting tasks will affect 80 % of your productivity

Ok, you get the idea. The point here is that you want to focus your attention, time, and resources on the students and activities that are producing the greatest results. Think about this scenario as you consider areas of your life where applying the 80/20 Rule would be beneficial.

The 80/20 Rule is a rough approximation, a guide. It's not a scientific law. It can be used to help you decide which activities are high priority or not worth doing at all. Pay attention to those tasks and activities which provide the greatest return. Eliminate tasks which contribute little or nothing to your success. Application of the 80/20 Rule will dramatically improve your productivity.

GET STARTED

Your dreams define your success. If you want to change something in your life then take action. Have you noticed that once you get started on a task, it's not as bad as you thought it would be? This happens because once you actually begin working on something important to you, you naturally become motivated to continue. There is a part of you that actually enjoys keeping busy doing things that make a difference.

Too many people waste time preparing to begin. Rather than starting, they spend countless hours planning and sometimes end up with no time left to complete the task. Don't spend too much time fussing over the details. Get started and do your best work with the resources you have. Stop wasting time thinking about what you are going to do and just start doing it. **Remember, it's the finish, not the start that counts!**

There comes a moment when you have to stop revving up the car and shove it into gear.

— *David Mahoney*

A LAURIE STORY

How Long Does It Take to Write a Book?

All the adversity I've had in my life, all my troubles and obstacles have strengthened me. . . . You may not realize it when it happens, but a kick in the teeth may be the best thing in the world for you.

— *Walt Disney*

I put off writing this book for about two years. It was not intentional; I just never took the time to get started. I finally accepted the fact I would not begin writing unless I changed my approach and did something drastic. I decided to announce to everyone with whom I came into contact that I was writing a book. This turned out to be a terrific idea because it created the positive pressure I needed to get started.

The positive pressure came from the questions I received from Dave, Margarite, and Freda. I would see these same individuals after prolonged periods of time and they would invariably ask:

"How's your book coming along?"

"What's the title?"

"What's it about?"

"Who is your audience?"

"Do you have a publisher?"

"When can I buy a copy?"

Since I had no answers, I kept my responses brief and simply replied, "It's coming along." I started to feel vulnerable and embarrassed when they would see me after a year or two and ask the same questions. I felt that they could tell I wasn't really doing anything, I was just talking. Because I didn't want to lose my credibility, I decided to eliminate the excuses and to develop a plan. I focused all my energy on the task of writing this book.

My familiarity with the 80/20 Rule taught me that 80 percent of the task was just getting started. With this in mind, I committed to getting up an hour earlier every morning. This was my way of making time, instead of finding time. I began the project by creating a detailed table of contents, and breaking each chapter into manageable sub-sections. This allowed me to finish each section I started. I forced myself to do whatever was necessary, even if it was something I didn't enjoy. I didn't put off doing unpleasant tasks. I made a choice to write a book and I knew I had to complete it in order to reach my goal.

When the project seemed too overwhelming and I didn't think I could complete this book, I would remind myself that finishing it was going to be a lot easier than having to announce to friends and relatives that I had quit. As you can see, I did it!

> *In the morning, I say: 'What is my exciting thing for today?'...Don't ask me about tomorrow.*
>
> *— Barbara Jordan*

Activity

Procrastination - This Can't Wait!

Identify your goals, priorities, values, strengths, opportunities, and weaknesses. Compare your actions to your goals and priorities. Are they consistent? One definition of insanity is to do the same thing over and over again and expect different results. Many of us want to change things in our lives. We talk about it but never seem to get up enough energy and motivation to make it happen. Here are some reasons why we may procrastinate. Check out the list below and add your own reasons to the list.

- Laziness
- Poor time management
- Anxiety
- Negative beliefs such as, 'I can't, I won't, I'm not, I lack'
- Finding the task boring, lack of interest
- Lack of clearly defined meaningful goals
- Perfectionism – constant planning but never taking action
- Fear of success
- Fear of failure
- Fear of criticism

Is there something you've been planning on doing but haven't gotten around to? What is it?

_____

Identify three reasons why you procrastinate. In the second column, write down what you will do to improve.

WHY	SOLUTIONS
1. _____	_____
2. _____	_____
3. _____	_____

List three ways you waste your precious time. Then list what you will do to eliminate each poor habit. Time wasting activities are things like: excessive television watching, gossiping, too much talking on the phone, consistent on-line surfing or chatting, unnecessary shopping, etc.

TIME WASTERS	SOLUTIONS
1. _____	_____
2. _____	_____
3. _____	_____

Time stays, we go.

— _H.L. Mencken_

OPPORTUNITY, COURAGE, FEAR AND RISK

Never be afraid to try something new. Remember, amateurs built the ark. Professionals built the Titanic.

— Unknown

Opportunity	An opening, a break, a chance for progress
Courage	The confidence of mind or spirit to face danger or fear
Fear	An uneasy feeling of agitation, anxiety, dread, or apprehension
Risk	The possibility of suffering harm or loss; uncertain danger

Life is full of opportunities. There are times however, when we don't pursue opportunities because we don't want to take any risks. Fear prevents many of us from acting with courage. Lack of courage causes many of us to simply accept and deal with what we already have, even if what we have is not what we want. The two Laurie Stories in this chapter reveal what's possible when we ignore our fears, act with courage, and seize opportunities.

☀ RICH CHOICES ☀

Opportunity, Courage, Fear, and Risk

- Seize Opportunities
- Be Courageous
- Ignore Your Fears and Do It Anyway
- Take Reasonable, Intelligent Risks

SEIZE OPPORTUNITIES

A friend of mine recently confessed that she wanted to go to college a get her bachelor's degree. When I asked her if she was going to pursue it she said: "No! It's too late and I'm too old. Besides, I'll be 38 by the time I graduate." I responded by saying, "God willing, you're going to be 38 anyway. You might as well have the degree on your 38th birthday." I'm not sure that's what she wanted to hear.

Sometimes we put obstacles in our own paths. It's bad enough when we use the opinions of others as an excuse for our limited, small-time thinking. In my friend's case, she didn't need any help, she created her own limitations. Opportunities abound yet many of us don't see them. We grow older and we think it's too late to try new things.

It's never too late to try something new. Explore new ground and seize opportunities at every step of your life. Don't put limitations on your dreams and goals. Everyday is full of amazing opportunities to learn new things. Each one of us has the innate ability to continually grow. The time is now!

BE COURAGEOUS

Courage is a state of mind. It's the ability to take risks without fear. It's your inner strength which allows you to face your fears with confidence. "Self-trust is the essence of heroism," wrote Ralph Waldo Emerson. Sometimes self-trust is what we need to be courageous. Eliminate doubt and try something new. Don't concern yourself with the activities and opinions of others. Instead, look deep within yourself for the guidance and strength that you already posses.

Shoulda, Woulda, Coulda! Don't go through life wishing you had done something. Our lives require excitement and adventure; this is what keeps us alive. None of us want to look back on life with regrets. There's an expression — act now, ask for forgiveness later. Eliminating self-doubt is the first step toward acting with courage. Be bold, be daring, be courageous!

IGNORE YOUR FEARS AND DO IT ANYWAY

Act in spite of your fears. Go ahead and take action! Do what you're afraid to do. Believe you can have whatever you want as long as you're willing to take some risks in order to obtain it! Fear is the great immobilizer; it is what prevents many of us from pursuing our goals. As we get older and become bogged down with life and its responsibilities, fear and uncertainty increase. Identify your fears and let go of them. Develop the habit of saying: "I'm afraid, but I'll do it anyway!"

Chances are you heard the expression, "Nothing ventured, nothing gained." Each of us goes through periods in our lives when we feel anxious, scared, nervous, or uneasy. This is natural. It is during these times when you simply have to face your fears in order to advance to the next level and to be your best. Be enthusiastic about your strengths, focus on what you know you can do, and imagine how great you're going to feel when you achieve your dream. Step out on faith and go for it. The world loves a champion.

TAKE REASONABLE, INTELLIGENT RISKS

Jumping off the roof of a skyscraper without a parachute is not considered a reasonable risk. That might be called just plain 'ol stupid. A reasonable or intelligent risk is one in which you try something new or different and the potential benefits are positive and rewarding. We admire and applaud individuals that we see as successful, but seldom do we consider the risks they took to get where they are.

Define the benefits associated with an intelligent risk. Size up a situation and determine if the benefits are worthwhile. If they are, then take a chance. You'll be better off in the long run and you'll be proud of yourself. This is how to achieve success in life. Little by little, intelligent risk taking will pay off. Go ahead and do something bold. Taken in doses, risk is good.

> *The first step in the risk management process is to acknowledge the reality of risk. Denial is a common tactic that substitutes deliberate ignorance for thoughtful planning.*
>
> — *Charles Tremper*

A LAURIE STORY

The Gregory Hines Story: When Courage and Opportunity Meet!

> *We should consider everyday lost in which we don't dance.*
>
> — *Neitzsche*

Authors' note: My life and the world of dance have been enriched because of one very special man, Gregory Hines. He was admired as a delightful and charismatic performer on stage, in film, and in television. An incredible tap dancer, actor, teacher, choreographer, mentor, humanitarian, and friend, he was generous with his talent and he will be missed tremendously.

The year was 1998 and I had just moved to Los Angeles, California. I met an employee at a casting company who suggested I work as an extra during my free days. Since I didn't have a job and had nothing but "free days," I figured, why not?

I've only worked as an extra twice in my life and this is my story. During my first experience, I wanted to watch the filming of the sitcom and those in charge preferred that I sit in a back room and wait. I was kicked off the set for challenging and disobeying the rules!

Working as an extra on the set of a sitcom is not glamorous, exciting, or fun. You spend your time waiting to shoot the scenes for which you've been hired. Anyone who has ever worked as an extra on a sitcom knows it can be frustrating.

One of the most challenging things I have ever done in my life was on the set of the Gregory Hines Show. On this, my second and final experience, I had to be careful not to break too many rules.

While on the set, I talked to as many staff members as I could. I mentioned to everyone I was a tap dancer. I am usually not that aggressive but I was on a mission. I asked if anyone knew of plans to include tap dancing on upcoming episodes. Finally, a staff member said he had heard something about a tap segment and suggested I speak with the director.

To seize the opportunity I would have to be bold; I would have to break the rules (again) and risk being kicked off my second set. I had already taken some risks and this was no time to stop. I made my way to the director and simply asked him if there were plans to incorporate tap dancing on future episodes. He informed me it was Gregory's call and suggested I speak with him.

I had worked with Gregory Hines in the past but was not certain he would quickly remember me. I did not want to waste time introducing myself and reminding him of our prior meetings. That would have been boring, predictable, and inefficient.

As I sat waiting with the other extras, I could see Gregory moving about the set. He was working on various lighting and wardrobe changes. I eagerly watched and waited as he traveled back and forth to his dressing room. I kept thinking about the consequences of being caught. Finally, I reminded myself the worst that could happen was my career as an extra would be over. That was sufficient motivation for me to take action.

I excused myself from my holding quarters (that's what it felt like) and waited in a small, narrow, dark corridor just outside Gregory's dressing room. I was really scared; I didn't know what I was doing. I knew one thing: he would have to pass me to get back onto the set.

When he finally opened the door, we were staring at each other. I quickly approached him and very clearly and confidently said, "I understand there may be a tap segment on one of your upcoming episodes. Is that right?" He replied "Yes", but did not break his stride. Just when he was about to pass me I shouted, "Gregory, check it out!"

He had no choice but to look; I was blocking his path. I couldn't believe what I was doing. I was tap dancing. I danced in front of him for about 15 seconds, giving my very best. All I thought about was how stupid I must look wearing a pair of green Doc Martens. That's right, green! I really didn't care how I looked. I had absolutely nothing to lose and a gig to gain. I stopped dancing and immediately asked, "So, Gregory, what do I need to do to get in on this gig?" He quickly resumed walking towards the set. He looked back, raised his arms, and shouted, "YOU JUST DID!" A week later, we began rehearsals and the episode aired within two months.

So what happened after the show aired? Absolutely nothing! I was not bombarded with hundreds of calls from industry professionals asking me to dance again on national television. I didn't get calls from agents asking if I needed representation. The only calls I received were congratulatory calls from friends and family. Rather than sit around waiting for doors to open – I decided to make something happen.

With the help of some friends, Belinda, Amalia, and Jennifer, I created a top notch demo reel which included clips of my solo dancing along with footage from the television show.

At that time, GAP (the clothing company) was airing dance commercials and I wanted to do a "GAP TAP" commercial. I spent a lot of time and energy creating that reel. I had a studio paint their walls, floor, and ceiling white so that I could replicate the GAP look. I created a video cover with letterhead that matched the GAP logo. I mailed several copies to their commercial producers and followed-up with phone calls. I eventually learned there were no plans to create a tap dancing ad.

I never did get to do a GAP commercial but my demo reel paid off in many other ways. Joe Tremaine and Julie Adler of Tremaine Dance Conventions were so impressed that they hired me immediately upon viewing it. I received lots of other opportunities as well. For many viewers, it wasn't a question of shall we hire her, it was a question of how much will we have to pay her? The demo reel is that good. You can check it out by logging on to www.lauriejohnson.com.

That day I forced myself to not worry about what "might" happen. The most difficult part was getting over my fear and getting up and doing something bold. I would never have forgiven myself if I had not taken that risk. I acted courageously and it paid off. Opportunity is everywhere and it's our responsibility to summon up the courage to break through our fears! Just think what I would have missed if I had not "TAPPED IN" to my full potential!

> *Plant the seeds of expectation in your mind; cultivate thoughts that anticipate achievement. Believe in yourself as being capable of overcoming all obstacles and weakness.*
>
> — *Norman Vincent Peale*

ANOTHER LAURIE STORY

My Experience on The John Walsh Show: I Think I'm Afraid!

> *What lies behind us and what lies before us are small matters compared to what lies within us.*
>
> — *Ralph Waldo Emerson*

My appearance on The John Walsh Show aired October, 2003. Many individuals asked me about that experience. My response was simply…"I've come a long way in two years."

The John Walsh producers found me through my web-site. They conducted an internet search using the phrase "quit corporate job." Fortunately a phrase or sentence on my website was a magnet. They were planning a show about people who quit their corporate careers to pursue their passions. When I received the phone call requesting my appearance on the show, I was delighted but scared.

You see, if I had been asked to do the show just two years prior, I would have lied and said I was booked. Two years ago, if the producers had asked me the day of the show if I brought my tap shoes, I would have lied and said "No, I'm sorry, I didn't bring my shoes." Actually, I would not have had to lie; I really would have left my shoes home so that my excuse would have been valid!

Just a few years ago I avoided taking some risks because I was afraid. Afraid of what people would say, afraid of not being good enough, and afraid of failing. These fears prevented me from taking risks and held me back. Here are some of the excuses I have used:

- "I'm not ready!"

- "My book is not finished."

- "I've gained a few pounds!"

- "My tap dancing is rusty, I haven't been practicing."

- "I don't have enough time to get ready!"

- "Who me? Why me? What have I got to say?

- "What if I say something stupid?"

- "What will people say?"

I could go on and on but you get the idea. Fear holds us back and we create excuses we BELIEVE to be true. A week before the taping of the show I had a tooth extracted and there was a big gaping black hole in my pearly whites. I seriously considered backing out and using this as my excuse.

I forced myself to let go of my fears and enthusiastically responded, "Yes, I would love to do the show and yes, I did bring my tap shoes with me, and yes, I would love to perform." It wasn't easy and I was still afraid, but I did it anyway. I acted in spite of my fears and I was able to move closer to my ultimate dream – to become a television talk show host.

Fear of failure and in some cases, fear of success is what prevents many of us from pursuing our goals. With each stage of uncertainty, the fear grows stronger. Dr. Joyce Brothers wrote, "The person interested in success has to learn to view failure as a healthy, inevitable part of the process of getting to the top." After the show aired, I felt confident and capable. I let go of my fears and I stopped worrying about what people would say. I developed the habit of saying: "I'm afraid, but I'll do it anyway."

Subsequent to my appearance on The John Walsh Show, I have done several other television interviews, a live radio broadcast, and I have been featured in various print media. Let's just say, I still have some work to do. Through these experiences I've learned what not to do when I appear on Oprah. Here are the Top Ten things I've learned:

10. Hire a stylist and/or carry my own foundation. Just because there's a make-up artist on-site doesn't mean they have my shade.

9. Memorize my "Passion Principles" because that's what people want to talk about.

8. Don't get caught glancing at the monitor to see what I look like on camera.

7. Don't interrupt the interviewer.

6. Listen to the question, formulate a response, and then speak.

5. Make sure the person responsible for typing the on-screen captions knows the difference between the words "Principles" and "Principals."

4. Only provide the show with footage that compliments me and speaks to my message.

3. Don't give 'em too much cleavage on a day-time talk show.

2. Sit up straight and give the impression I'm relaxed and enjoying myself.

1. Ask to hear the music I'm going to dance to – before the show starts.

The saddest words of tongue or pen are these four words – it might have been.

— Oliver Wendell Holmes

Activity

Pull Yourself Together!

Think back on a time when you really wanted to achieve something. Trying out for a sports team, a dance audition, getting a promotion, passing an exam, etc.

Write down the event or activity.

_____

Answer the following questions:

Did you seize opportunities?

_____

Did you take any reasonable risks?

_____

Were you afraid?

_____

If you were afraid, how did you deal with your fear?

_____

Did you act with courage?

_____

Write down the event or activity:

_____

_____

_____

_____

_____

It is better to be prepared for an opportunity and not have one than to have an opportunity and not be prepared.

— Whitney Young, Jr.

GOT FORGIVENESS

Holding on to anger is like grasping a hot coal with the intent of throwing it at someone else; you are the one who gets burned.

— Buddha

When someone causes us pain, we may find it hard to forgive and to let go. We hold on to the pain and the negative emotions that result because we've been hurt or have been treated badly. Sometimes we feel justified in our anger. Our hope is that the other person is suffering from our disregard for them. This is wrong. When we think in these mean, negative ways, we are only hurting ourselves. Holding on to negative thoughts and emotions contaminate every area of our lives.

 **RICH CHOICES**

Got Forgiveness
- Protect Your Mind And Heart By Letting Go of the Small Stuff
- Forgiveness is an Act of Strength, Not an Act of Weakness
- What About When You're The One Who's Wrong
- Do Unto Others…

PROTECT YOUR MIND AND HEART BY LETTING GO OF THE SMALL STUFF

Research shows that forgiving those who hurt us can help us manage anger, reduce stress, improve our mood, and get better sleep. Carrying around bitterness and resentment is toxic. Holding on to anger and having thoughts of vengeance tears at the core of our being.

We are the one who suffer when we choose to hold on to self-destructive and negative emotions.

When we're unwilling to let go of anger, the negative emotions and thoughts don't remain specific to just that one event. Negative emotions that start with one situation transfer to other aspects of our lives, and before long, we're angry at everything and everybody. What starts in your mind transfers to your heart; negative emotions contaminate other parts of you. When you're unwilling to forgive, you contaminate your mind, your body, and your soul.

Valuable time and energy spent concentrating on someone we dislike or someone we believe has hurt us, causes us to be unproductive. While you should not let anyone disrespect you, you don't need to waste energy being negative. By developing the habit of letting go of the small, insignificant things, you clear your mind of negative clutter. When we move past the petty stuff, negative emotions surface less frequently and with less intensity. Accept your family and friends for who they are. Love them unconditionally. Bring your best self to the relationship at all times; that's all you can control.

FORGIVENESS IS AN ACT OF STRENGTH, NOT AN ACT OF WEAKNESS

Forgiveness and letting go might sound like giving up, but it isn't. It is an act of strength and it is the path to freedom. To achieve our full potential and to maintain a positive outlook, we must let go of the small stuff in life. It's unproductive to hold on to self-destructive, negative energy, and to simultaneously try to be positive in other, select areas of our lives.

Forgiveness doesn't just happen. It requires a conscience decision on your part. Your life will become more peaceful and gratifying as you develop the habit of letting go of things outside your control. With your newfound sense of freedom you will be able to move on to more important things in life. Things like focusing on your dreams and goals.

Forgiveness is not easy, but it is necessary. It's something you do for yourself, not for someone else. Freeing yourself from negative thoughts and emotions that result from letting go is a power only forgiveness can provide. Be strong and take the high road; act from a place of strength, not weakness.

WHAT ABOUT WHEN YOU'RE THE ONE WHO'S WRONG

It is simply a waste of time being stubborn and not wanting to admit when you're the one who's wrong. The energy spent denying and blaming would be better spent if you simply admitted your wrongs and moved on. It doesn't make you less of a person or a loser to do this. On the contrary, it makes you a bigger person. You'll be amazed at how quickly others will let go of their anger once you say, "I'm sorry, I was wrong. I'll work on getting better." It sounds so simple doesn't it? That's because it is that simple.

Understanding where and how you went wrong is the first step. Oftentimes we say we're sorry without understanding why. When two children have a disagreement, adults have them apologize without ensuring that they understood what they did. Make your apology sincere, and learn from the experience. It won't be as painful to admit to your mistakes next time. Make it a habit to take responsibility for everything you do. When you're the one who's wrong, admit to it, and get on with the business of making your life an exciting success.

DO UNTO OTHERS...

We all have the same basic needs. We want to be loved, understood, and we want to feel connected to others. When we feel connected to others, we treat them as if they are a part of ourselves. When we feel separate from others we are more self-centered and focused on ourselves. Feeling connected eliminates some of the negative judgments and negative feelings that result when we feel disconnected from others.

Remembering that we all have the same basic needs allows us to truly live by the golden rule: "Do unto others as you would have them do unto you." Act, respond, and live as if you are connected to everyone with whom you come into contact, because you are.

Motivation is what gets you started. Habit is what keeps you going.

—*Jim Ryun*

A LAURIE STORY

Forgiveness – The Antidote to Anger!

That old law about an eye for an eye leaves everybody blind. The time is always right to do the right thing.

— *Martin Luther King, Jr.*

I was 22 years old and I remember how I felt as if it happened yesterday. I was working as a customer service supervisor at a telecommunications company. I was hired along with another employee, whom I'll call T.B. T.B. and I were the same age, were hired on the same day, worked the same hours, held the same job title, and had the same responsibilities. I had an advantage over T.B. because I had a college degree. He had a high school diploma.

T.B. and I spent a lot of time together. We attended all the same meetings, conferences, seminars, workshops, and training sessions. Because we enjoyed each others company, we even went to lunch together. During the first seven months on the job, T.B. and I became friends.

One day, PAY DAY, to be specific, T.B. innocently began talking about how much of his pay had been deducted for taxes. He felt comfortable doing this because he assumed we were making the same salary. I noticed his taxable amount was a lot higher than mine. It was then I discovered his annual salary was $9,000 more than mine.

T.B. grew embarrassed while I became disgusted, outraged, and disappointed. I think he felt the carpet burning as I turned to leave the room. I was furious.

This was one of those situations when I didn't need to think about what to do. I didn't need to go home and cool off, nor did I need to get anyone else's opinion. I simply walked into my manager's office and closed the door behind me. I felt rage in my heart but I remained cool and confident. My only thought was "nobody treats me this way."

I spoke to my manager in a very calm manner. I told her I just learned that my colleague was making more than me. I didn't need to go into details about our job responsibilities and credentials. She knew the deal. I told her I was confident she would remedy the situation before COB (close of business). I made it clear I wanted this resolved quickly so we could all get back to business. I did not wait for her response; I wasn't in the mood for an apology or an excuse.

A couple of hours later she called me into her office and apologized for the "discrepancy." That's what she called it. I kept thinking 'I don't like to be disrespected.' I was just glad she took my earlier advice and quickly remedied the situation. I received back pay for the previous seven months and my salary was corrected.

I politely thanked her for her timely response and left her office. I didn't gossip with anyone about what happened. To do so would have been unproductive and disruptive. I figured what good could come from gossiping and complaining? Besides, I don't complain to people who are not in a position to help.

I was shocked at the courage I displayed that day. There was no confrontation on my part, just a statement of the facts and a request for what I wanted. I forgave the management and gathered their respect in return. During the next couple of months I became actively involved in implementing new policies to end pay scale "discrepancies" like I had experienced.

In this instance, I made the decision to forgive and to move on. I didn't want a court battle. Forgiving helped prevent negative thoughts and emotions from taking over my heart and mind. I learned that things external to me have no power over me, unless I let them. Letting go of the small, insignificant things helped me to clear my mind, made me powerful, and allowed me to focus on my future possibilities.

> *I look to a day when people will not be judged by the color of their skin, but by the content of their character.*
>
> — *Martin Luther King, Jr.*

Activity

No More Resistance!

Find a quiet spot to sit and consider the following questions:

How easy is it for you to let go of your resentment or frustration?

_____

What does it feel like when you hold on to your pain and pride?

_____

The next time you find yourself mentally holding on to a grudge or to anger, think about what you can do to release it?

_____

_____

What benefits will you achieve by letting go of the hurt, pain, worry, remorse, and expectations? Put it in writing.

_____

_____

The weak can never forgive. Forgiveness is the attribute of the strong.

— Gandhi

RELATIONSHIP INVENTORY

A true friend stabs you in the front.

— *Oscar Wilde*

CRITICISM CAN DESTROY AMBITION

- "Who are you to aim so high?"
- "What if it doesn't work?"
- "What qualifies you to write a book?"
- "What do you know about the philosophy of money?"
- "Do you really think you can do that?"
- "What will you do if you don't succeed?"
- "People will think you're crazy!"

If you ever find yourself in the company of someone who asks you these types of questions, get away from them quickly. Associating with negative people is draining. Additionally, negative influences destroy your ambition and your desire to achieve.

IF YOU WANT TO SOAR WITH EAGLES, LEAVE THE PIGEONS ALONE.

THE THREE KINDS OF PEOPLE

Here are some hard, fast, simple rules about the three kinds of people:

Growth

Growth people are energizers. They are people you trust, admire, and respect. They are friends who give you good advice and honest feedback. They tell you the truth even if it hurts. When you are in their company, you feel like you can accomplish anything. Growth people are the ones to reach out to when you are in need. You can improve your life and your attitude by choosing to spend more of your time with people who can help you grow.

Neutral

Neutral people are those individuals who have no impact on who you are. Store clerks, letter carriers, and tollbooth attendants are all examples of neutral people. If you never saw them again – it would not make a difference, your life would not change.

Toxic

Toxic people are battery drainers. They are underperformers, pessimists, whiners, and cynics. Don't waste your valuable time thinking or complaining about them. They can't handle the success of others so they set out to embarrass, demean, or control. Toxic people don't belong in your life. They will always try to find a way to make you feel bad or guilty. The most difficult thing to accept about toxic people is the fact that they can be family members. There is only one way to deal with a toxic person: limit your interaction with them. If you have to be in their presence, be polite and make yourself scarce. You will accomplish in life only what you believe you can. Associate with positive, growth people.

☀ RICH CHOICES ☀

Relationship Inventory
- Limit Your Interaction With Toxic People
- Surround Yourself With Growth People

LIMIT YOUR INTERACTION WITH TOXIC PEOPLE

We tend to take on the nature and habits of those with whom we associate. Associating with toxic people makes us think and respond to life negatively. It is not your responsibility to do what others expect of you, but what you expect of yourself.

SURROUND YOURSELF WITH GROWTH PEOPLE

Associating with positive, growth people raises our level of thinking and helps us to become more ambitious. People who care about you are not intimidated by you. They appreciate and respect your uniqueness. They encourage and inspire you to be your best. As a result, you will take risks and achieve more.

The greatest gift we possess is the power of choice. Choose wisely!

Some people cause happiness wherever they go; others whenever they go.

— *Oscar Wilde*

A LAURIE STORY

Running With the Big Dogs!

There are two great rules of life, one general, the other particular. The first is that everyone can, in the end, get what he wants if only he tries. The particular rule is that every individual is more or less an exception to the general rule.

— *Samuel Butler*

Growing up I often heard expressions like:

- If you can't run with the big dogs, stay on the porch.
- If you want to soar with eagles, leave the pigeons alone.
- If you lie down with dog's you'll get up with fleas.
- Birds of a feather flock together.

None of these adages had much impact on me until I had graduated from college. It was then I realized the impact the company I kept had on me and how much we tend to take on the thoughts and attitudes of those with whom we associate. While working at a telecommunications company in Washington, D.C., I had the privilege and honor of working for a man who became my mentor, Nate Davis. Here is an actual letter I sent to him several years after I left that company.

Dear Nate,

Thanks for the kind words and the compliments, I'm glad you liked my website. Nate, although it's been several years since I left your employ, I think of you often. I give a lot of motivational talks and invariably I mention your name. I talk about your unwavering ethics and your high moral standards. I site specific situations and tell how you handled yourself during the period of time I worked for you. You were relentless and maintained very high standards.

You were – and you continue to be – my mentor. Hard to believe isn't it? Yes, it's true. Although we don't speak very often, I'm frequently reminded of your ethics, integrity, and honesty. To this day I remember how well you conducted yourself in meetings and behind the scenes. I knew you were honest from the way you conducted business and from the way you managed your employees. In your eyes, a dollar was a dollar, corporate or otherwise. There was never any suggestion or hint of impropriety on your part. It was from your actions, not your words, that I learned many valuable lessons. You were thorough, conscientious, and honest.

You continue to play a major role in shaping my life. Lest we forget, it was you who told me I needed to formalize my education and get my master's degree. Back then, I didn't even know what you were talking about. (I had my moments, huh?) I pursued my MBA because you told me I needed to. It was just that simple for me.

When I am confronted with a difficult situation, regardless of whether it's related to business or to daily life, I think about you and try to handle it as you would. I especially try to lead by example. Isn't it funny how we impact the lives of others without realizing our power and influence?

I am so grateful for the opportunity to have worked with you. More importantly, I am grateful for the example you set. You held me accountable for my actions and to a high moral and ethical standard. Now I know what my mom was trying to tell me when she would continually say "If you can't run with the big dogs, stay on the porch."

Yours in love and dance,
Laurie

It's obvious from this letter I respect Nate for his leadership and for his ethics. Working for him taught me the value of associating with positive, growth people. When it comes to the company you keep, the bottom line is this: Those who are worthy of being in your life will not be threatened by your strengths, uniqueness, and talents. They will encourage you to be your best and to do your best.

Hold fast to dreams for if dreams die, life is a broken-winged bird that cannot fly.

— *Langston Hughes*

Activity

Mapping Your Social World!

Make a map of your social world. Put yourself in the center, and then draw lines to family members, friends, coworkers, classmates, teachers, and spiritual leaders with whom you interact regularly. Categorize each person in your circle according to the RELATIONSHIP MATRIX (Growth, Neutral, or Toxic).

Your Name Here

Any surprises?
With whom in your family are you closest?

_____

What part do you play in helping to keep this relationship healthy?

_____

Nearly every friendship has it ups and downs. We each need different things at different times in our lives.
What friendships do you need to let go of temporarily?

_____

What friendships do you need to let go of permanently?

_____

What does being a friend mean to you?

_____

How could you be a better friend to others and to yourself?

_____

Which of your friendships need improving?

_____

What action could you take today to heal a relationship that is declining?

_____

Henceforth I ask not good fortune. I myself am good fortune.

— *Walt Whitman*

DESIGN YOUR LIFE
WITH PASSION

There has never been another you. With no effort on your part you were born to be something very special and set apart. What you are going to do in appreciation for that gift is a decision only you can make.

— *Dan Zadra*

Have you ever watched someone accept an award and during their acceptance speech they talk about how fortunate they are to do what they love and get paid for it? What crosses your mind when you hear someone say they are paid to live out their dreams and passions? Do you think they're lucky? Do you wonder if your life could ever be so terrific? Yes, it can!

Luck is what happens when preparation meets opportunity.

— *Seneca*

How do you design your life to get what you really want? First, you must know what it is you want. Many adults find their passion in the things they did as children. My sister Mary, is a wonderful example of someone who found her passion early in life. She has been a dancer, an instructor, and a studio owner. Currently, she is founder and owner of Imagine the Impossible Dance Workshop in Dallas, Texas, a non-profit organization that inspires and motivates inner city kids through classical ballet training. Mary shares her love of dance with thousands of dancers each year and is admired for her passion and for her belief that dance enhances children's lives.

Education is our passport to the future, for tomorrow belongs to the people who prepare for it today.

— *Malcolm X*

Our passions are the things we enjoy doing; they give us energy and a sense of destiny. It's what we were born to do. You are a unique individual and you are the only one who can fulfill your destiny. There has never been another individual like you and there never will be. Pay attention to what brings you joy - that could very well be your passion. Designing a life based on your passions is not easy, but it is necessary.

Make it a point to live completely and to make good use of your talents, abilities, and opportunities. We all have unique abilities, talents, and interests. Every one of us has a purpose for being here on earth. God gave each of us a gift and our gift, in return, is the proper use of our abilities. Our responsibility is to identify our gifts and talents, then use them to help others and ourselves.

Do not wish to be anything but what you are, and try to be that perfectly.

— *St. Francis de Sales*

☀ RICH CHOICES ☀

Design Your Life With Passion

- Dream Big
- Be Willing to Try New Things
- View Failure as a Learning Tool
- Cut Your Losses
- Manage Your Thoughts
- Think Like A Free Agent
- YOU – Make It Happen
- Use All Your Resources
- Ask For What You Want
- Go For It

DREAM BIG

If you can't see it, you can't get it. Your mission in life is to make your dreams come true and to help others do the same. Instead of worrying about your future, visualize yourself in the future and focus on your possibilities and your talents. Dream big and be prepared to work hard. Moreover, remember: a dream without a goal is simply a wish. Believe in yourself. You were created to make your dreams come true.

> *We must look for ways to be an active force in our own lives. We must take charge of our own destinies, design a life of substance and truly begin to live our dreams.*
>
> *— Les Brown*

BE WILLING TO TRY NEW THINGS

You are the architect of your life. No one can take your passion from you except you. In designing your life - challenge yourself, try something new. You can only succeed by taking reasonable risks. Reasonable risk-taking is good and you'll feel great when you succeed. Keep in mind, you risk as much, if not more, when you do nothing. Take passionate action towards designing your life.

> *Behold the turtle. He makes progress only when he sticks his neck out.*
>
> *—James B. Conant*

VIEW FAILURE AS A LEARNING TOOL

There comes a time in all our lives when we fail at something. My eye-to-hand coordination was so poor I could never hit a baseball, tennis ball, or volley ball. I felt like a loser because that's what I was called by my classmates. Back then I didn't understand that failure was a learning tool. Don't accept mediocrity in life. When we're unwilling to risk failure we create a life that is safe, conventional, boring, and ordinary. The real winners in life are willing to tolerate failure, identify errors, take responsibility, and make corrections. If you've never failed at anything, you've never risked anything.

Failure is only postponed success... The habit of persistence is the habit of victory.

— *Herbert Kaufman*

CUT YOUR LOSSES

A U-Turn Is Better Than No Turn. The lyrics of a popular old country song say: "You've got to know when to hold 'em and know when to fold 'em." Sometimes we may be reluctant to get out of a bad situation or investment because we've invested so much time, money, or effort into it. There may be times when your best course of action is to cut your losses and to make the correction. If you're in a bad situation and know you're heading in the wrong direction, don't fear the criticism of making the correction. A dead end is a good place to make a u-turn. If you don't admit to your mistakes and faults, you can't make the correction. The more you get used to owning up to your shortcomings, the better you will become at dealing with them when they occur. Try to turn problems into opportunities. When you realize you've made a mistake or a bad decision, cut your losses, make the correction, and get back on track. Those of us who learn and grow from our missteps are the true winners in life.

Forgive yourself for your faults and your mistakes and move on.

— *Les Brown*

MANAGE YOUR THOUGHTS

Your life is all that's really yours, all that you own. The only security you have in this world is the management of your own thoughts. You will never accomplish more in life than you believe you can. Commitment and dedication are essential to achieving personal success and fulfillment in life. Your time spent here on earth is precious and it is your thinking and your attitude that determines your experience. Your thinking makes it so.

The world we have created is a product of our thinking; it cannot be changed without changing our thinking.

— *Albert Einstein*

THINK LIKE A FREE AGENT

The job market isn't what it used to be. Years ago people graduated from high school or college and asked themselves: "How will I make money?" Many simply took jobs and kept them for years. Oftentimes the prize was a gold watch at retirement after 20 or more years of service. Today it's different. Instead of asking "How will I make money?" we're asking: "How do I go about discovering my true self and using my skills to better myself and others?" Today, we're free agents who have the opportunity to design our own careers. Begin thinking about your passions and come up with creative ways to design your life around your skills. Don't settle for a life in which you squeeze your skills into somebody else's definition of a job.

There are hazards in anything one does, but there are greater hazards in doing nothing.

— *Shirley Williams*

YOU – MAKE IT HAPPEN

Every year thousands of young adults move to Los Angeles or New York hoping to pursue a career in the entertainment industry as an actor or dancer. Many of them develop the habit of waiting. They wait for an agent, producer, or choreographer to call them announcing their "dream job." More often than not, it doesn't happen. This is one of the many areas where self management is critical. Just as we nurture our bodies through proper exercise and nutrition, we must also properly nurture our thoughts, our emotions, and our time. No one else is going to make your dreams come true; you must be an active force in your life. You must demonstrate an ongoing commitment to achieving your goals. Think creatively and take action.

Even if you're on the right track, you'll get run over if you just sit there.

—*Will Rogers*

USE ALL YOUR RESOURCES

Research indicates that most of us are getting by using just a tiny percentage of our brainpower. Research also reveals that people's number one fear is having lived a meaningless life. It must be horrible to grow old and to have deep regrets about the choices we've made. Some of us don't accomplish all that we're capable of simply because we don't work hard enough. Maintain a positive vision of yourself and continually strive to improve your consciousness. Use all your skills and talents so that you live in peace and not in regret.

To say yes, you have to sweat and roll up your sleeves and plunge both hands into life up to the elbows. It's easy to say no, even if it means dying.

—*Jean Anouilh*

ASK FOR WHAT YOU WANT

People like to feel needed. If you have a friend who can help you achieve a goal, ask for their help. When others see you consistently taking action towards self improvement, they will gladly provide assistance.

Friends are quiet angels who lift us to our feet when our wings have trouble remembering how to fly.

—*Author unknown*

GO FOR IT

Once you know what you want, the next step is to dedicate yourself to making it a reality. You are worthy of all that life has to offer.

Focus, commit, and persist. We live in a world of abundance. You can have all you desire, as long as you help others get what they need and want. Make a difference, leave a legacy. The world will step aside for the person who knows where they are going!

> *It is not the critic who counts, not the man who points out how the strong man stumbled, or where the doer of deeds could have done better. The credit belongs to the man who is actually in the arena; whose face is marred by dust and sweat and blood; who strives valiantly; who errs and comes short again and again; who knows the great enthusiasms, the great devotions, and spends himself in a worthy cause; who, at the best, knows in the end the triumph of high achievement; and who, at the worst, if he fails, at least fails while daring greatly, so that his place shall never be with those cold and timid souls who know neither victory nor defeat.*
>
> *— Theodore Roosevelt*

As you read these rich choices, you may find you are already living with them. If there are areas where you can do better, do it. Doing just one thing better every day will significantly improve your future.

> *Take care, don't fight, and remember: if you do not choose to lead, you will forever be led by others. Find what scares you, and do it. And you can make a difference, if you choose to do so.*

> — *J. Michael Straczynski*

A LAURIE STORY

Tapping Into Wealth: How I Turned My Passion for Tap Dancing Into a Career!

> *If you put a small value on yourself, rest assured that the world will not raise your price.*

> — *Author unknown*

In the past, I was a marketing executive at a Fortune 500 company. Armed with an MBA from one of the nation's top business schools, my corporate career path was staged. Before age 30, I had consummated a salary deal in excess of six figures. And while I liked the money, I loved tap dancing even more.

Tap dancing had always been my passion but I rationalized no one was about to pay me to tap dance all day long. So I quit my job and in 1997, began my crusade to earn a living as a full-time tap dancer. Now I travel around the world, dancing, lecturing, and inspiring others to pursue their passions.

Throughout my travels, I've met a lot of people and I'm asked a lot of questions. The questions I am most frequently asked are as follows:

Question: Why did you leave the corporate world?

Answer: I truly believe that each of us can create the life we desire. I did not want to live my life feeling like a coward. The worse fate for anyone is to grow old and look back with regrets; to wish they had taken more risks. I knew that if I did not leave my job I would be disappointed with myself, and I would end up spiritually and emotionally unfulfilled.

I also wanted more peace in my life. The amount of energy I spent earning a living and juggling the demands of home and career were exhausting and unfulfilling. Corporate life was stifling. At the end of the day

I felt empty and my life lacked meaning.

Question: How did you come to the decision to tap dance?

Answer: My mother once told me that when deciding on a career, I should choose something that I do well and that I enjoy. She firmly stressed that I must choose something I do well. She told me not to concern myself with money, that money would follow hard work. I knew I was a talented tap dancer. It took me a while to convince myself that I could be successful as a dancer, because initially, it sounded so ludicrous. Despite all my doubts, fears, and anxieties, I tapped into my faith and stepped out.

Question: What kept you motivated? How did you stay positive and focused during the difficult periods?

Answer: Mark twain said, *"Nothing is really work unless you'd rather be doing something else."* I posted this quote onto my office computer and read it several times a day. The more I read it, the more I came to realize I was compromising my values and my life for a paycheck in corporate America.

When I resigned, I did not know what I would do. I knew that if I continued to wait around for the perfect plan, nothing would ever happen. I had to take a risk and I reminded myself I was taking a risk on the one thing I trusted – myself. That, coupled with my faith in God, gave me the necessary strength and courage to make my first and most difficult move.

Question: What advise do you have for people who want to pursue their dreams but don't know how to get started?

Answer: Create freedom for yourself by creating options for yourself. This is best done while you're young. Go to college, gain some work experience, save your money, find a mentor, surround yourself with Growth people, and limit your interaction with Toxic people. By establishing options you give yourself the freedom to take more risks.

To add meaning and purpose to our lives we must be willing to risk exploring the things about which we feel passionate and enthusiastic. More than anything, we need courage. We can have what we want when we stop making excuses, and giving our power away. Who we are at the core of our being cannot be ignored; it speaks to us through our body and spirit.

If you want something, you have to be willing to take some risks. Begin by taking small steps. Focus on the rewards and benefits that will result.

No one knows what is best for you better than you do. No one cares about you as much as you do. Ignorance of who we are and what we want is what makes us settle for unnecessary pain and suffering. The power to transform our lives is our own responsibility. When we don't use our God-given power, we lose courage and confidence, and life becomes a daily struggle.

Man is only truly great when he acts from his passions.

— *Benjamin Disraeli*

Activity

Are You Passionate?

On a scale of one (don't think much about it) to ten (enthusiastic), how passionate are you about your future?

List five things you're really passionate about. In the next column jot down why you like each one. Putting your passions in writing will help you focus on them.

Passions	Why?
1.	
2.	
3.	
4.	
5.	

List five goals you're looking forward to achieving. What actions could you take today to get started?

Goals	Actions
1.	
2.	
3.	
4.	
5.	

The man who does not work for the love of work but only for money is not likely to make money nor find much fun in life.

— *Charles Schwab*

LAURIE'S PASSION PRINCIPLES

Happiness includes chiefly the idea of satisfaction after full honest effort. No one can possibly be satisfied and no one can be happy who feels that in some paramount affairs he failed to take up the challenge of life.

— Arnold Bennett

I truly believe each of us can create the life we desire. The reason so many of us are in emotional, financial, and personal turmoil is because we are ignorant of who we are and what we want. Peace and serenity continue to elude us because we spend our time trying to please everybody else and because we judge ourselves by standards set by others.

To transform our lives we must first be willing to accept responsibility for its current condition. Any person with courage, who knows what he or she really wants to do, can change his or her life from failure and boredom to success and contentment.

Every one of us has a purpose for being here. Our life's work is to discover that purpose and then to pursue it with passion. I developed the following **Passion Principles** as a guide to help you discover, develop, and create a healthier, more meaningful life. These **Passion Principles** helped me transform my life from one of mediocrity and boredom to one filled with growth and discovery.

The **Passion Principles** will help you create the life you dream of. Start identifying your passions, the things you enjoy doing and the things you do well. Define your actions, clarify your purpose, and get a real clear vision for your life. All of us have God-given talents and natural abilities. It is our responsibility to use our talents and other natural resources to create a life filled with joy, prosperity, and peace.

The life you desire is the life you deserve.

RICH CHOICES

Laurie's Passion Principles

Passion	–	Ignoring Your Passion is Like Dying In Slow Motion
Preparation	–	See It, Name It, Claim It
Performance	–	Opportunity is Everywhere, Be Prepared
Persistence	–	Persist and You Will Prevail
Prosperity	–	Do What You Love and It Will Give You Abundance in All Forms, Including Money
Peace	–	Make Sure What You Do Serves Yourself and Others

PASSION

Ignoring Your Passion is Like Dying in Slow Motion

In life, we are producing only a fraction of what we really want. The way to true success is to honor our passions and talents. We can transform our lives the moment we become aware of who we are and what we want. Who we are at our core cannot be ignored or denied. When we do not take the time to self explore, we end up settling for limited lives, lives filled with unnecessary pain and suffering. Determine what you are passionate about and begin the process. Stop waiting for something outside yourself to make something happen in your life. Stop giving your power to others and to activities that sap your creative energies. The struggle is a mental one – not to give energy to fear, criticism, negativity, or failure. Ignore your naysayers. *The life you desire is the life you deserve.*

PREPARATION

See It, Name It, Claim It

Break through every pattern of: *"I can't,"* or *"I shouldn't,"* or *"What will happen if I do?"* Ask yourself how would you like to be living this time next year? Five, ten, twenty years from now? Name it, and begin laying the foundation to claim it. Part of your planning requires commitment and unwavering dedication to your vision. With this commitment comes an understanding you will face failure, criticism, and rejection. You must remain disciplined, focused, and persistent. Plan your work and then work your plan. *The life you desire is the life you deserve.*

PERFORMANCE

Opportunity is Everywhere, Be Prepared

So what, you failed a couple of times. Work through it, get over it, and get back to it. Failure is inevitable. Pay attention to your pain. It is through pain and self-reflection that we begin to see ourselves more clearly. Sometimes our insecurities make us pretentious and defensive. Let down your guard and be honest with yourself. Next, be willing to make changes, otherwise, there can be no improvement. In the Chinese language, the word "crisis" means opportunity. Let failure and crisis serve as a turning point and as an invitation from God to grow. Opportunity is everywhere. *The life you desire is the life you deserve.*

PERSISTENCE

Persist and You Will Prevail

How we experience life always reflects our thoughts, words, and actions. Our feelings and choices are created by our beliefs – beliefs we have the power to change. What is needed to make the shift is courage – the courage to love, to know who you are and what you want. Make a decision to believe in a better life and work to attain it. Do what makes you feel energized, connected, and stimulated – you will triumph! *The life you desire is the life you deserve.*

PROSPERITY

Do What You Love and It Will Give You Abundance in All Forms, Including Money

Prosperity is our birthright. Too often, we think small and have even smaller expectations. As we make positive changes in our attitude and actions, the doors to prosperity will begin to open. Do not compromise your values to make money. Honor your highest self; pursue your passion and you will be rewarded with ever-increasing prosperity. ***The life you desire is the life you deserve.***

PEACE

Make Sure What You Do Serves Yourself and Others

No one knows what's best for you better than you do. No one cares about you as much as you do. When we do not use our God given talents and resources, we demean ourselves, we lose courage and confidence, and life becomes a daily struggle. Decide to celebrate life by living it joyfully. With a positive mind-set, you can decide not to be at war with life but at peace with the everyday. Make a decision to eliminate thoughts of fear, criticism, negativity, and failure. Your responsibly to your life's work is to find your life's work. Ask yourself: What do you want to be? Then hang up the phone, turn off the television, close the magazine, and do what you have to do. ***The life you desire is the life you deserve.***

A LAURIE STORY

Go Ahead, Tell Me I Don't Have What It Takes!

A man found an eagle's egg and put it in a nest of a barnyard hen. The eagle hatched with the brood of chicks and grew up with them. All his life the eagle did what the barnyard chicks did, thinking he was a barnyard chicken. He scratched the earth for worms and insects. He clucked and cackled. And he would thrash his wings and fly a few feet into the air. Years passed and the eagle grew very old. One day he saw a magnificent bird above him in the cloudless sky. It glided in graceful majesty among the powerful wind currents, with scarcely a beat of its strong golden wings. The old eagle looked up in awe. "Who's that?" he asked. "That's the eagle, the king of the birds," said his neighbor. "He belongs to the sky. We belong to the earth – we're chickens." So the eagle lived and died a chicken, for that's what he thought he was.

— Anthony De Mello

Are you a golden eagle unaware of the heights to which you can soar?

I have always known I was different. Different because I've always believed I deserved nothing but the best. Regardless of my circumstance or my surrounding, I've never appreciated being told "No" or being overlooked. Since I thought I deserved the best, I never settled for less. Many people accept less than the best because they don't believe they are worthy of more. Their thinking is limited, just like the eagle in the above story.

When I decided to get my masters degree I knew I wanted to attend a top business school. I graduated from George Washington University with my undergraduate degree. I was working my way up the "corporate ladder" at a telecommunications company. One of my goals was to become a corporate officer and getting an MBA (Masters of Business Administration) was the logical next step towards achieving this goal. I understood the value of a degree from a reputable institution.

I obtained a list of the top ten schools and applied to each of them. I was very confident I would be accepted. Since I figured I would be going to school in August (1992) I quit my job in June. I planned to enjoy the summer and to prepare for my academic journey. I figured wrong. I ended up having 14 months off instead of three!

The first nine response letters all began the same way, "We regret to inform you." I held out hope for that tenth *acceptance* letter. Unfortunately, it too said the same thing, "WE REJECT YOU." I was not devastated, I was shocked. My initial response was not "what's wrong with me?" Instead, it was "what's their problem, what's wrong with them, don't they know who I am?" I thought there had been some sort of mistake.

Quantitative skills? What's up with that? I didn't know I needed background coursework in accounting, statistics, finance, calculus, and micro and macro economics. WHO KNEW? I found this out by speaking with several admissions officers. They all concurred. I was not accepted because I needed a lot of prep work.

In addition to taking college level courses in the above areas, I needed to retake and improve my score on the GMAT (Graduate Management Admissions Test). Additionally, I was informed I needed to start reading periodicals like The Wall Street Journal, The Financial Times, and The Economist. The Economist? I had never even heard of it.

Several admissions officers told me that even if I was accepted, there was no way I could do the work. My thought: "How do they know what I can do?" This rejection fueled my desire to succeed even more. I was energized by being told "No, you don't have what it takes to make it." Imagine someone, anyone, informing you of your abilities. Rejection ignited my desire and provided me with ammunition. I thought, "I'll show them!"

I was not willing to accept defeat. Although I was embarrassed and sad, I reminded myself that feeling bad was temporary, defeat was forever. I made a commitment to do whatever it took to get into graduate school.

I began by going to the library six days a week for a minimum of six hours a day. For the next 12 months I packed a lunch and left for the library every morning. Bringing lunch prevented me from leaving the library and from wasting time. It also helped me to save money. I was unemployed, on a tight budget, and on a mission. Fortunately I had some money saved and of course, I earned a little extra money teaching tap classes during the evenings.

The following year I re-applied to the same ten schools. I was rejected by nine. Did I care? No! I could only go to one school so I only needed one yes. I received it from The University of Texas (Austin). They accepted me "ON CONDITION." This was their way of informing me I was a risk. I was accepted on the condition I maintain a B average. If I did not, I would be dismissed from the two year, full-time program.

Upon completing the first semester I received a letter in the mail. It said, "You have been dismissed!" My GPA (grade point average) was too low. Again, I refused to have my future controlled by forces outside myself. I was not about to leave the school I had worked so hard to get in.

It's at times like this when we must not accept defeat. When the world is telling you: "No, you can't, you're not, and you won't," you've got to believe you can and you will. You have what it takes to make your way in the world, as long as you believe you do and are willing to work to make it happen.

Here's what I did: I wrote a letter to the Dean of the business school detailing my plan to improve my grades. I followed up by scheduling a meeting with him. During the meeting, I presented my case and asked for another opportunity. I outlined my plan to improve my grades. I listed very obvious things like purchasing a computer, studying with groups, enhancing my organizational skills, visiting professors, and getting extra help. My approach worked. He agreed to allow me to remain in the program on the condition I put my plan into action.

Just before leaving his office, I decided to be bold. The toughest part of the meeting was over and I had nothing to lose. I informed him of my financial situation. I told him I was experiencing financial hardship and asked if there was anything he could do to help. Without making any phone calls or putting up any resistance, he said "Done!" He immediately authorized the reduction of my tuition by 50 percent by making it possible for me to pay in-state tuition rates. Hooray! Another hurdle overcome by simply asking for what I wanted. I completed the rigorous academic program and I graduated on time, with an MBA from a top business school.

The lesson? Don't let anyone tell you what you can and cannot do. Take pride in whatever you do and aim high. Be bold and be willing to ask for what you want. People will respond to you based on your level of confidence. Be proud, stand strong, and know that you deserve the best. You are a golden eagle. I want you to realize the heights to which you can soar. Be aware of your greatness.

> *If you don't go after what you want, you'll never have it. If you don't ask, the answer is always no. If you don't step forward, you're always in the same place.*
>
> *— Nora Roberts*

Activity

Your Passion Fashion!

Make up your own quote or tag line for each of the six Passion Principles.

PASSION_____

_____

PREPARATION_____

_____

PERFORMANCE_____

_____

PERSISTENCE_____

_____

PROSPERITY_____

_____

PEACE_____

_____

The distance is nothing; it's only the first step that is difficult.

— *Marquise du Deffand*

BOOK TWO

FINANCIAL MANAGEMENT

FINANCIAL GOAL SETTING

Make no mistake, my friend, it takes more than money to make men rich.

— *P. Gouthey*

Where are you now? Where do you want to be in the future? How do you get there? There are different types of goals. Some of your goals may be personal, others financial. Goal setting is the process of identifying what you want and when you want it. Goal setting provides direction to your life. It gives you a way to measure your progress, and helps you focus your energy on important things.

Do you live each day with a worthy financial goal in mind? Can you vividly see yourself achieving your financial goal? Do you imagine what you'll feel like when you reach it? Your financial goals are a reflection of your needs and values.

Each of us will have a different set of financial goals. Take the time to write yours down, and be specific. Remember, vague goals produce vague results. Putting your financial goals in writing will help you to outline a plan for achieving them. Small goals = small rewards, large goals = big rewards! Keep your mind on the payoff!

☀ RICH CHOICES ☀

Financial Goal Setting

The key to effective goal-setting is to make sure your financial goals are:
- Specific
- Realistic
- Flexible
- Measurable
- Meaningful

SPECIFIC

Goals are specific things you want to accomplish within a certain period of time. List your objectives concisely and outline your specific strategy for how you are going to reach your goals. Be specific and set a deadline for achieving it. If your goal is to avoid getting into credit card debt, then you must commit to paying off your balance in full each and every month, no excuses. Unclear goals won't be meaningful and will be hard to achieve.

REALISTIC

Your goals must be realistic; otherwise you may become frustrated and abandon your plans. If one of your financial goals is to save money, perhaps it's unrealistic to save $100 a month right away. Plan to save $25, and then gradually increase the amount.

FLEXIBLE

Plans change. As things in your life change, you may be required to make adjustments to your plans. Don't be so rigid that you have to

start over with a whole new plan. Stay on track. If something comes up unexpectedly, deal with it and get back to your plan. Continue to work towards your goals.

MEASURABLE

Set benchmarks or targets so you can measure your progress. It's a great feeling to look back and to see how well you've done. Keep in mind that reaching a long-term goal may depend on achieving several short-term goals along the way. Plan a small reward for each segment achieved then a king-size reward for the big targets achieved.

MEANINGFUL

Choose goals that are meaningful to you and that get you motivated. Identifying meaningful goals is the key to achieving them. A meaningful goal is one that is significant and worthy.

> *Time is like money, the less we have of it to spare the further we make it go.*
>
> *— Josh Billings*

A LAURIE STORY

Change is Good!

Restlessness is discontent and discontent is the first necessity of progress. Show me a thoroughly satisfied man and I will show you a failure.

— *Thomas Edison*

Bad habits can be broken. However, eliminating poor financial habits and replacing them with rich choices requires commitment and practice. It is only this past year that I finally developed the habit of counting my change after making a cash purchase. This is a lesson I learned the hard way.

On several recent occasions I received incorrect change from store clerks. I would discover this (several) hours later when I realized that I didn't have as much money stuffed in my pockets as I thought I should. After a few of these instances it became apparent to me I was being short-changed. I decided not to dwell on why store clerks were giving me incorrect change. Instead, I focused on the only thing over which I had control; my actions. Here are some of the reasons why I didn't count my change:

- I was in a hurry.
- I didn't want to hold up the line.
- I felt self-conscious while counting change in public.
- I wasn't in the habit of counting change. I used a credit card for most of my purchases.
- I didn't have a wallet in which to organize my money.
- I didn't want a wallet. I carried a very slim card case containing my license and a credit card.

Without a wallet, I simply stuffed money into my pockets or a bag. I had to find a way to eliminate this poor, self-defeating habit. The rich choice was simple: get a wallet and count my change. I purchased several wallets over a period of time, but none of them met my needs. I quickly fell back into my old, poor habit. The end-of-year holidays were approaching and my good friend Joelle Martinec, who was not aware of my poor habit, presented me with a gift.

What do you know? It was a wallet, and it met all my requirements. It was cute, feminine, just the right size, held a couple of credit cards, and was in one of my favorite colors, lime green. How many times have I thanked her? I'm still thanking her. Today, I am no longer short-changed. I successfully eliminated a poor habit. I quickly count my money while organizing it in my wallet. Thanks, Joelle!

> *Annual income twenty pounds, annual expenditure nineteen six, result happiness. Annual income twenty pounds, annual expenditure twenty pounds ought and six, result misery.*
>
> — *Charles Dickens*

Activity

My Financial Goals!

Here are some suggestions of worthy financial goals:
- Successfully managing a credit card and/or checking account
- Committing to your budget
- Saving for college
- Getting your own place
- Consistently balancing your check book
- Eliminating or avoiding debt
- Improving cash management skills
- Saving and investing for your future
- Saving money to purchase a new toy, computer, electronic game, auto, etc.

List three of your financial goals. Then write down the actions you will take to make your goals a reality.

Goals

1. _____

2. _____

3. _____

Actions

1. _____

2. _____

3. _____

Are you currently doing any of these things?

_____

Part of your heritage in this society is the opportunity to become financially independent.

—Jim Rohn

RIGHT ON THE MONEY – SUCCESSFUL BUDGETING

Prepare! The time will come when winter will ask what you were doing all summer.

— Henry Clay

Budgeting is an ideal way to make your financial goals a reality. A budget is a tool for saving and spending; it helps you to know where your money is going and keeps your spending in perspective. **A budget is your best planning device.** Budgeting helps you to manage spending by establishing spending limits. In addition to helping you to focus on your goals, budgeting helps you to distribute your resources among competing goals.

You can set up your budget by the week or by the month. Start by identifying your income and your expenses. Income is money earned or given to you. Expenses are things like school supplies, books, cell phones, calculators, clothing, rent, tuition, auto payments, gas, and insurance. If you have money left over you're in great shape. You can decide to increase your savings or spend money on less essential things like entertainment, electronic gadgets, and cosmetics. If your expenses exceed your income, then you will need to decrease your expenses or earn more money. Creating a budget helps you to determine how much money you have coming in and going out.

HOW YOUR CASH FLOWS

Cash Flow is simply the flow of money in and out of your life.

Money coming in = Income

Money going out = Expenditures

 Fixed Expenses = Regular, consistent expenses
 Variable Expenses = Flexible expenses

Fixed Expenses – Some of your expenses will be easy to record because they are the same every month. These are called fixed expenditures. Fixed items are things like rent, insurance, and auto payments. You still need to include them in your budget so you can see at a glance how much of your income is committed to current or future expenses. This also helps you avoid spending money on items not in your budget.

Variable Expenses – Variable expenses are items over which you have some degree of control. This is where you really get to test your ability to control and reduce your spending. Tracking your variable spending helps you identify patterns or habits that may stop you from reaching your goals. If, for instance, you notice your "miscellaneous" expenses continually increasing, you'll be able to catch it before you blow your budget.

SAMPLE MONTHLY BUDGET

On page 133 is a sample monthly budget I helped create for Ashley. Ashley is a high school junior who wants to save $3,000 over the next two years for college expenses. She earns money teaching seven tap classes a week at a dance studio. She earns extra money rhine-stoning costumes for the studio's competitions and recitals. Ashley is on her school track team and she often needs money for running shoes and other equipment. She lives with her parents so she has no household expenses. Ashley had already reached her first goal; she purchased her father's used car for $6,000 and has 4 years to pay it off.

Before Ashley begins her monthly budget, she needs to know her monthly financial commitments. Then she'll determine how much she wants to save each month and over what length of time.

Tip: To identify the amount to save each month, Ashley divided the total amount of money she wanted to save ($3,000) by the amount of time (24 months). $3000 ÷ 24 months = $125 per month.

ASHLEY'S BUDGET

GOAL: Save $3,000 over 2 years for College Expenses

Net Monthly Income	Amount	Monthly Expenses	Amount
Teaching at studio – 7 classes a week at $15 each class = $105 / week. *To convert weekly income to monthly income, multiply by 4 weeks. Example: ($105/week x 4 weeks = $420).*	$420.00	Savings★ ($3000 ÷ 24 months = $125/per month)	$125.00
Tutoring 5 hours a week at $10.00 each hour = $50/week. *Monthly income = $50/wk x 4 wks = $200/mo.*	$200.00	Car Payment ($6000 ÷ 48 months = $125/per month)	$125.00
Allowance $30 per week	$120.00	Auto Insurance	$50.00
		Gas	$80.00
		Cell Phone	$25.00
		Clothes	$50.00
		Entertainment & Food	$135.00
		Credit Card Payment	$100.00
		Miscellaneous Expenses: Auto maintenance Laundry, dry cleaning Running shoes Magazines Cosmetics Books & school supplies	$50.00
Total Income:	**$740.00**	**Total Expenses:**	**$740.00**

★ *Savings is money identified by Ashley's goal. It is subtracted from income as soon as her paycheck is received.*

RICH CHOICES

Right on the Money – Successful Budgeting

- Establish Financial Goals
- Record Your Income
- Prioritize and Record Your Expenses
- Develop a Savings Plan
- Use the Plan

ESTABLISH FINANCIAL GOALS

Ashley knew exactly how much money she wanted to save and over what period of time. It's very important that you have a definite goal or purpose at which to aim. A major cause of failure in life is not knowing what we want. Establish a worthy goal and put it in writing. Choose goals that get you excited, and then you'll be more determined to reach them within your timeframe.

RECORD YOUR INCOME

After identifying her goal, Ashley gathered all her paycheck stubs and other income receipts to begin the budgeting process. She completed the income portion of the budget by adding all her income together and subtracting a percentage for savings. Her goal is to save $125 each month and her monthly income is $740. She wants to save 17 percent of her income. That's 125 ÷ 740 = 17%.

PRIORITIZE AND RECORD YOUR EXPENSES

Ashley recorded all of her known and expected expenses in the expense portion of her budget. Prior to setting up her budget, Ashley kept a spending log for several months. A spending log is a tool for tracking and monitoring cash spending. There is a sample log included in this book in the next chapter on Intelligent Consumption. Ashley's spending log helped her to identify expenses she may have missed or forgotten during the budgeting process. Prioritize your expenses by listing the most important items first.

Develop a Savings Plan

Ashley determined in advance that she wanted to save $3,000 over a two year period. This meant she needed to save $125 a month (3,000 ÷ 24 months). Some people have higher expenses than income. If this is your situation, you need to cut back on some of your expenses. Decide how much you want to save and begin the budgeting process.

Use the Plan

To reach your goals while paying for everyday expenses, you must have some sort of budget. For a budget to be effective, it must be used every day. Ashley kept up with her budget and tracked all her expenses. She did not exceed her budgeted amounts and she successfully reached her savings goal.

Before you begin to work out your plan, remember good money management starts long before you begin tracking dollars and cents. Your budget is a very personal issue. No one can tell you what your needs or desires should be. Only you can decide how to manage your financial life. Effective money management will depend on your choices and on the goals you set for yourself.

From now on when you think about spending money, consider your goals. Instead of going into debt, make a pact with yourself: Before I go to college, get my own place, go on vacation, and purchase a new computer or automobile, I will have the money to pay for it! Create a budget and put your plan into action. Start today! Launch your new plan with enthusiasm and make a commitment to reach your goals. When you do reach your goal, you'll feel a great sense of accomplishment and pride. Develop the habit of budgeting and monitoring your spending. Practice it daily.

The future belongs to those who prepare for it today.

— Malcolm X

A LAURIE STORY

I Was Broke, But I Wasn't Poor!

We must never be afraid to go too far, for success lies just beyond.

— *Marcel Proust*

During my last two years of college I transferred to George Washington University in Washington, DC. I rented a room in a neighborhood crammed with corner stores, dollar stores, and liquor stores. I lived there because the rent was cheap and it was close to school, and to my job on Capitol Hill.

The high cost of city living took its toll on me. I impulsively sold my car for $600 cash. I sold it on a whim and didn't think about alternate transportation. I ended up riding my bike to work and to school, regardless of the weather. One day, while riding home from school, I was hit by a car and knocked to the ground. On impulse, I jumped up and began hopping around. There were several witnesses to the accident. Among them was a group of men who spent their days hanging out on street corners doing nothing. They ran towards me shouting, "Sister, lay yo' ass back down so you can get paid!" I didn't crawl back down on the ground because that was not my mentality. I wanted to be healthy because I had things to accomplish.

My thinking has never been to look for handouts or to take unfair advantage of unfortunate situations. I was more concerned with the fact that I wasn't wearing a helmet. While in the ambulance, I was concerned about which hospital I was going to. You see, when you're in a poor, inner city neighborhood and you don't have medical insurance, things don't look so promising. I eventually had to have knee surgery to repair the damage caused by the accident. This left me on crutches for a couple of weeks. I was unable to tap dance or do anything else.

Looking back, this was by far one of the most difficult and depressing times of my life. I was miserable because of the accident, and because of my way of life. I was living in survival mode. I:

• Rode the bus to school and to work

• Shopped for groceries at expensive corner stores

- Used payphones and phone cards for all my calls

- Washed my clothes at public laundromats

- Rented furniture from "rent to own" places

- Cooked my meals on a hotplate in my small, dingy, ugly room

- Paid high fees to cash my paycheck at check cashing places

- Needed a co-signer for all my credit (utilities and rent)

- Paid my bills with money orders

- Traded regularly at local pawn shops

I went to pawn shops because I could always get cash by selling a neck-lace or a camera (on loan). I would then buy the item back for a few extra dollars when I got money. My life was horrible.

I may have been broke, but I was not poor. In fact, I was rich. I was rich because I didn't think like my neighbors. I had the good fortune to be a full-time student and a congressional intern on Capitol Hill. I lived in two very different worlds.

At home, I struggled on a daily basis just to make ends meet. While at school and work, I was surrounded by individuals whose primary concerns were getting good grades or promotions and investing in their financial futures. My neighbors didn't have access to this other world like I did. My neighbors were poor. They were focused on buying the next item that would make them feel good about themselves: expensive clothes, hair extensions, flashy jewelry, trendy accessories, and high-end cars. I quickly learned what I didn't want for my future. My neighbors didn't have the opportunities I had. I saw what was possible.

On a recent trip to New York, I saw one of my cousins. She is 15 years old. She asked me for $20 dollars. I asked her how much money she had saved. When she said, "Five dollars," it was obvious to me that she had misunderstood my question. I grinned and said, "No, I mean, how much money do you have SAVED?" She casually replied, "Yeah, I have five dol-lars and I'm saving that to get my nails done." I stared at her, wanting to believe she was joking. Deep down, I knew she was serious. I was speech-less, something that doesn't often happen. I felt horrible.

My cousin thought and acted like my earlier neighbors. She was focused on instant gratification with no vision of her future. I explained to her that she was spending a lot of time and energy maintaining her external self and doing very little to develop her inner value and self-worth. I concluded by telling her she was doomed to a shallow life if she didn't start to think and behave differently. She didn't have to say a word. Her facial expression and body language said it all. She was thinking, "Ok, I listened to whatever you just said – NOW will you give me the money for my manicure?"

I understand her thinking very well. Throughout my life I've been around people who think this way. They are poor, but they are not powerless. They are NOT living in poverty. Poverty is a different issue. The US Census Bureau defines poverty as an "economic condition in which people lack sufficient income to obtain basic needs for food, housing, clothing, health services and education."

My cousin is surrounded by poor people whose primary concern is consumption. These individuals always want more and are willing to spend money to make themselves feel important. They would rather spend their last couple of dollars on a new pair of sneakers than invest or save. They don't realize that what they own does not give them status or make them better.

My cousin focuses on instant gratification because she doesn't have a vision of her future. No one has ever talked to her about it. She doesn't realize that college is a possibility for her. No one tells her what she can accomplish. No one tells her that she is important. No one's eyes light up when she walks into a room.

She is constantly reminded of her limitations. Every day she is bombarded with images and messages that, by design, remind her that she is nothing without the latest, most expensive, clothing, jewelry, hair, etc. In her particular case, I know why she spends all her money so quickly on herself. If she didn't, her family would know she had it and ask for a loan. This mentality keeps this horrible cycle spinning.

I will continue to talk with my cousin. I don't want her to stay poor and broke. I want her to know what she can achieve. I want to make sure she has the tools to make intelligent and informed financial decisions. When she starts working and gets an increase in salary, I want to make sure her first thought is to invest the extra money, not to impulsively spend it on some worthless, insignificant, disposable nonsense.

Unless you know what you want, you can't ask for it.

— Emma Albani

MY BUDGET WORKSHEET

MY GOAL:

Net Monthly Income	Amount	Monthly Expenses	Amount
Job Income	$	Savings★	$
Other Income	$	Expense	$
Allowance	$	Expense	$
		Expense	$
		Clothes	$
		Entertainment and Food	$
		Credit Card Payment	$
		Miscellaneous Expenses: 　Auto maintenance 　Laundry, dry cleaning 　Cell phone 　Magazines 　Cosmetics 　Books & school 　　supplies	$
Total Income:	**$**	**Total Expenses:**	**$**

★ *Savings is money subtracted from income as soon as your paycheck is received.*

I've got all the money I'll ever need, if I die by four o'clock.

— *Henny Youngman*

Activity

Budgeting – Making Ends Meet!

Think of all your income as a pie. If you cut one piece too big, all of the other pieces will have to be cut smaller. Consistently overspending means you won't have enough money to cover your expenses. Everyone can't use the same budget or plan. You are special and different from every one else. Your needs, wants, values, and resources are different. You should manage your money to get what you need and to maximize the benefits from your income. Establish a worthy goal and set up a budget to help you achieve that goal. Don't delay, get started now!

Refer to the sample monthly budget included in this chapter and begin to think about your own budget. Keep in mind that as your life changes, your budget will change. The purpose of budgeting is to help you reach your goals, not to force you to conform to rigid rules. Don't be discouraged if your budget doesn't work out right away. You may have to revise it several times. Continue to review it from time to time to be sure it is consistent with your goals.

Complete the "My Budget Worksheet". Then determine which of the following three scenarios you fall into:

1. **Your income and expenses balance.**
   Congratulations! You're on the right track. This is a great way to stay on budget.

2. **Your expenses are greater than your income.**
   This means you're spending more money than you have – it's decision time! Reprioritize your expenses and decide what needs to go. Perhaps you'll need to skip a trip to the movies, or go without a manicure in order to decrease your expenses.

3. **Your expenses are less than your income.**
   This is a good position to be in. Decide what you want to do with the extra money. You can add more money to your savings or to the biggest priorities in your budget. You may decide to reward yourself by buying something you've been wanting.

Start where you are with what you have, knowing that what you have is plenty enough.

— Booker T. Washington

INTELLIGENT CONSUMPTION

Action without planning is fatal, but planning without action is futile.

— *Tracie Van Eimeren*

If I gave you $100 it is very likely you would spend it differently than your friends, your parents, or me. Think about what you would do with the money. Answering this question is important because it will help you to understand why you spend your money the way you do. Everyone will most likely spend it in entirely different ways. Why? Because we're all different and we value things differently.

For the most part, values are not right or wrong; they simply reveal what is important to you. A major reason why so many families, friends, and couples argue about money is because their values and goals are different. Your values are deeply rooted ideas about what you believe is good. Your beliefs result from your personal experiences. Your goals are based on your values, and how you spend your money is a reflection of your values.

You can make your money go further through proper and careful financial planning. Now that you have set meaningful financial goals and created a budget, you're ready to move on to the next level. Next you must plan, control, and monitor your spending. You must make intelligent consumption choices to meet your goals, to stay within your budget, and to build your financial future.

 **RICH CHOICES**

Intelligent Consumption

- Ask Yourself: Do I Need It or Do I Want It
- Walk Away
- Identify Your Spending Triggers
- Avoid Impulse Purchases
- Comparison Shop
- Learn to Say "NO"
- Don't be Pressured by Aggressive Sales Tactics
- Think Before You Spend
- Consider Using Other People's Money
- Maintain a Spending Log to Track Your Cash (Out) Flow

ASK YOURSELF: DO I NEED IT OR DO I WANT IT

Do you spend more money on things you need or things you want? Have you ever thought about the difference? Understanding the difference between *necessities* and *niceties* is critical to establishing good spending habits. Before making a purchase, develop the habit of asking yourself: "Do I need it or do I want it?" Eliminate excessive spending on items that add little value to your life or to your future. **Don't put today's wants before tomorrow's needs.**

NEEDS: Needs are basic items required for your personal safety and your health. Needs are things like food to nourish your body, clothing to keep you warm, and shelter to protect you.

WANTS: Wants are things not critical to life. Tattoos and jewelry are not required for your personal safety; they are wants. Wants are just that, things we prefer and desire for our pleasure.

Remember, to reach your goals and to afford the items you need, you can't spend all your money on things you want.

WALK AWAY

Stores are carefully designed to get you to spend more. Walking away is an ideal technique for developing the habit of keeping your money in your pocket. If you see something you want, take a moment to consider how the purchase will benefit you long-term. Is it in your budget? If not, consider walking away. Walking away gives you time to re-consider the purchase or to let the impulse to purchase pass. Sometimes walking away causes you to become distracted by other wants. You may realize you're simply shopping out of boredom or emotion. So go ahead, wander off and get your money to wander off with you.

IDENTIFY YOUR SPENDING TRIGGERS

Some of us are emotional spenders. We shop to celebrate when things are going well and we shop to make ourselves feel better when things aren't going so well. Shopping then becomes a way to achieve immediate gratification, temporary moments of happiness and excitement.

Emotions account for a lot of spending and retailers know this. They spend time and money figuring out what you will buy and they develop clever techniques to attract your interest. Why do you think candy in the supermarket is at the eye level of young children? If you want to spend less and save more, avoid exposing yourself to things that will tempt you to spend! Shopping should not be your hobby, find something else to make you feel good. Take a dance class.

AVOID IMPULSE PURCHASES

Stores are carefully designed to get you to spend money. Some stores place complimentary items together in the hopes you'll spend more. Ever notice that the pasta is close to the sauce and cheese, beer is close to pretzels, coffee is close to cream, and salsa dips are close to chips? Shopping with a list is a great way to monitor spending and control impulses. If an item is not on your list, leave it. Don't develop the impulse spending habit. Eliminate the habit of indiscriminate spending. The roads that lead to riches and poverty travel in opposite directions.

COMPARISON SHOP

Before you decide to buy, be sure to comparison shop. Comparison shopping is especially important for larger, more expensive purchases. Gather reliable and accurate information and then compare the alternatives. Remember, the prices on electronic goods drop very quickly. If you can wait, you'll save money.

LEARN TO SAY "NO"

Once in a store you can't remove the temptations, so control your response to those temptations. Know your limits. If an item is too expensive for your budget, or doesn't rank high on your spending priority list, leave it alone. Most importantly, don't buy from your friends or relatives selling products just because you feel obligated. You don't need to provide excuses. Keep it simple and just say, "I can't," "no-thanks," or "maybe another time."

DON'T BE PRESSURED BY AGGRESSIVE SALES TACTICS

Remember, salespeople exist for one reason and one reason only, to sell you the goods! If an item is in the store today, chances are it will still be there tomorrow. Give it some thought. Perhaps the purchase will not be as appealing later. Don't be pressured by aggressive sales techniques and fancy marketing pitches.

THINK BEFORE YOU SPEND

When you're tempted to spend money, stop, think, and ask yourself the following questions:

- What are my financial goals and what are my priorities?
- Is this the best use of my money right now?
- Is this a budgeted item or an impulse purchase?
- Can I wait and buy it later? Perhaps it will go on sale.
- Is the price negotiable?

- Is there a substitute for this item? Perhaps I already have something I can use.

- Can I make it instead of buying it?

- Will I use the item just once?

- Is this something I can borrow or rent?

CONSIDER USING OTHER PEOPLE'S MONEY

For those who just love to shop – consider using other people's money. Begin a shopping service for friends, family, and neighbors who don't enjoy it or who don't have the time. My cousin, Carol, does this. She makes money by shopping for birthday, anniversary, and holiday gifts for friends and family members. She charges a fee for her time and energy. She created a money-making opportunity for herself by doing something she enjoys.

MAINTAIN A SPENDING LOG TO TRACK YOUR CASH (OUT) FLOW

Some of us have difficulty saving money because we run out of it so quickly. Oftentimes, we have no idea where it went. We find ourselves broke and have nothing to show for our money. An excellent technique for alleviating this problem is to monitor your cash spending with a Spending Log.

Track your cash spending for a minimum of four weeks. Use pencil and paper, a PDA (Personal Digital Assistant), or a journal. Carry it with you at all times and record your spending. Don't omit anything. You want to account for every penny spent. At the end of each of the four weeks, examine and total your spending by category. This will help you identify your patterns, trends, and habits.

148

SAMPLE SPENDING LOG

Date	Item Purchased	$ Amount	Need, Want, Impulse	Planned Purchase

Maintaining a spending log will help you answer the following questions:

- Have I developed poor spending habits?
- Am I doing pretty well and do I have a good handle on my spending?
- Am I getting the most for my money?
- Are there certain "triggers" that make me spend?
- Do I make a lot of impulse purchases?

Smart financial management means getting the most for your money. Examining past spending habits is one of the best ways to see where you may need to make changes in your future spending. To develop sound financial management skills you need to know where your money is going. Creating and maintaining a Spending Log is simple and easy. It's a simple thing to do but very few people take the time to actually track their daily spending. This might be a hard job for some people; others will find it very worthwhile and rewarding. No matter how you feel about it, it is an essential step towards sound financial management. Invest the time now for a better payoff later.

A LAURIE STORY

I Got Booted!

If I were to begin life again, I should want it as it was. I would only open my eyes a little bit more.

— *Jules Renard*

I went to college in Washington, D.C. where the parking enforcement rules were extremely strict and aggressively enforced. I began to receive parking tickets and chose to put off reading the small print on the backs of the notices. When I did finally read the policies, the payment due dates had passed and the $25 fines had doubled.

Rather than cut my losses and pay the increased amount, I procrastinated further. Eventually my car was booted. This meant that a lock was placed on the wheel of my vehicle making it impossible for me to drive. I was then required to pay all the increased parking fines plus extra fines for the removal of the boot. Additionally, every day I put off making a payment I was charged more in fines and penalties.

I spent countless hours waiting in lines to make payments and to claim my car from the impound lot. My procrastination cost me wasted time and money. This expensive lesson taught me to face my responsibilities early on.

The difference between stupidity and genius is that genius has its limits.

— *Albert Einstein*

Activity

Your Values – Ch-ching, Ch-ching, Ch-ching!

Try this activity: Read over the list below.

Place a "1" next to the items **VERY** important to you.

Place a "2" next to the items **SOMEWHAT** important to you.

Place a "3" next to the items that are **NOT** important to you.

Category	Rating
Automobile	
Body piercing and tattoos	
Books	
Candy, snacks, junk food	
Clothing	
Cosmetics & toiletries	
Cultural events	
Eating out	
Electronic gadgets and equipment	
Facials, massages, manicures, pedicures	
Gifts	
Health & fitness activities	
Home ownership	
Investing	
Jewelry and accessories	
Movies	
Music	
Paying off debts	
Saving money	
School supplies	
Sporting goods and events	
Vacation	

Can you tell what kinds of activities or things you value? Do your values match your financial goals? Review the items where you placed the number "1." If you spend a lot of money on these items, ask yourself if this money could be saved or used towards something more valuable.

Our life is frittered away by detail... Simplify, simplify.

— Henry David Thoreau

Stop Spending, Start Saving

Maturity is the ability to do a job whether or not you are super-vised, to carry money without spending it and to bear an injustice without wanting to get even.

— *Ann Landers*

Regardless of where you are in terms of saving money, chances are you could do better. Sometimes we buy things that add little or no value to our lives. These frivolous purchases move us further away from our financial goals and stall our savings. The best way to save money is to spend less. Do you have any self-defeating spending habits you want to change? Would you like to increase your savings? Do you often wonder, "Where did all my money go?"

☀ RICH CHOICES ☀

Stop Spending, Start Saving

- Pay Yourself First
- Think Like a Saver
- Keep the Change
- Bank on Your Future with an Automatic Savings Plan
- Don't Confuse Sacrifice with Deprivation

PAY YOURSELF FIRST

Commit to saving a percentage of your income. When planning your budget, plan for savings first. This is the way to create wealth. Here's an idea you might want to try. Before paying any bills or spending any money, decide on an amount to pay yourself first. I recommend starting with at least 10 to 20 percent of all your income. When calculating income, be sure to include allowances, gifts, odd jobs, and money from an employer.

Deposit 10 to 20 percent into a savings account before making any spending decisions. This is a great system for developing the habit of saving money. It also provides you with a systematic way to make your money grow. Don't fool yourself into believing you can wait until the end of the month and then put away what's left. There probably won't be anything left to save. Besides, why procrastinate?

THINK LIKE A SAVER

Savers know there's no such thing as disposable income. Savers don't fritter away money on recreational shopping, and they don't shop because they're having a bad day and want to make themselves feel better. Savers are not tempted by a sale. In fact, they often walk away from one. When savers do spend money, they ask themselves:

• Do I really need this?

• Can I do without this?

• Where can I find this item for less money?

• Can I substitute something I already have instead of buying it new?

Think like a saver and remember – there's no such thing as disposable income.

KEEP THE CHANGE

There's an expression, "Watch the pennies and the dollars will take care of themselves." Change is money too, and you must respect it just like you would any other currency. At the end of each day, empty all your change into a change jar. At the end of the month or year, roll the coins and put them into your savings account. You will be amazed at how quickly the change adds up. I bet you could easily save $10 to $30 a month by saving all your change. I know teens that save hundreds of dollars a year by simply emptying out their pockets at the end of each day into their own change jars? Oprah Winfrey's Angel Network, a charity organization, has raised millions of dollars annually by collecting change from its contributors.

Bank on Your Future with an Automatic Savings Plan

Have your bank automatically deduct money from your deposits and put into savings for you. You can also arrange to have your paycheck directly deposited into your account. These are great features for those individuals who have not yet developed the discipline to save on their own. Not only does Direct Deposit save you time, it saves you money. Some banks reduce or eliminate monthly fees for Direct Deposit accounts. Contact an officer at your bank and have them explain to you how to jump-start your savings.

Don't Confuse Sacrifice with Deprivation

One of the primary ways to reach your financial goals is to understand what it means to sacrifice. Consider the following scenarios:

- Skipping a movie with friends because you need to study for an exam.

- Not blowing your budget at the mall because you're saving to buy a new computer, a car, or something else you really want.

- Sitting with your friends in a restaurant, and being conscious of the price of different foods on the menu because you'd rather save your money.

Do these situations make you cringe? Do they make you think only about the fun you're missing? Many of us fail to reach our goals because we confuse sacrifice with deprivation.

Sacrifice is choosing to give up something of value for the sake of having something more important or worthy.

Deprivation is having a possession or enjoyment taken away. Deprivation makes us only think of ourselves and makes us focus on what we can't have.

Sacrifice focuses on a goal; it allows you to see something beyond today. If your goal is to save money to purchase a new car or electronic item, then you can't indulge all of your wants. Instead, you MUST make a conscious choice to give up something of lesser value right now (immediate gratification) in order to have or gain something far more valuable in the future (delayed gratification).

If you don't identify a meaningful goal or purpose, your sacrifices will indeed be nothing more than deprivation. Once you know what you want and have committed to doing what it takes to get it, you'll feel good about making the necessary sacrifices. It's not enough to simply identify goals; you must prioritize them and make the commitment to do whatever it takes to make your goals a reality.

Sacrifice requires self-discipline. Once you understand the difference between needs and wants, sacrifice and deprivation, you're well on your way to achieving your goals. Sacrifice is a wonderful concept when it's associated with a purpose. When sacrifice is connected to a goal or a purpose, the goal becomes more valuable than the sacrifice itself. You won't be as tempted to stop pursuing your goals as you would if you were trying to survive deprivation. Viewing sacrifice in this way makes it easier to achieve your goals because you won't feel like your depriving yourself. With practice, you will begin to see the connection between small sacrifices and great rewards. You can have anything you want over a period of time, but not at the same time. Decide what you want and do what it takes to get it. Stay the course.

A LAURIE STORY

Pobody's Nerfect!

Before you speak, listen. Before you write, think.
Before you spend, earn. Before you invest, investigate.
Before you criticize, wait. Before you pray, forgive.
Before you quit, try. Before you retire, save.
Before you die, give.

— *William Arthur Ward*

I was 22 years old and hadn't saved a penny. I had just graduated college and started my first "real job." I had been working for about six months when I received a promotion and a $9,000 raise. I called home to tell mother the good news. Her immediate response was, "That's fantastic! How much money do you have in your savings account?" I confessed that the thought of saving money had not even occurred to me. In fact, I didn't even have a savings or a checking account. With that, she instructed me to open an account and to begin saving. She said it didn't matter in the beginning whether I saved $5 or $50 each week. All that mattered was that I get started and save consistently. She finished by saying that once I began to see my savings grow, I wouldn't want to touch it.

What do you know? She was right. It felt good to have money in the bank. Once I saw my savings grow, I developed a sense of pride and ownership. I have continued to save since that time and have developed the "savings habit."

> *When a man says money can do anything, that settles it: he hasn't got any.*
>
> — *George Bernard Shaw*

Activity

No More Cash in the Trash, Please!

If you want to avoid developing poor money habits or are looking to improve your existing habits, there are several things you can do. One is to identify areas where you waste money — usually for instant gratification. Check out the list below. Can you find areas where you waste money? Identify your spending leaks by placing a checkmark next to all that apply.

Do You:

- ❑ Buy items to impress others or to brag?
- ❑ Buy items you know you can find cheaper elsewhere because you don't want to wait?
- ❑ Drop all your change into tip jars?
- ❑ Regularly pay an exorbitant mark-up on bottled water when you're away from home?
- ❑ Buy a second pair of shoes because a salesperson announced, "Buy one and get the second pair 50 percent off?"
- ❑ Buy coffee, soft drinks, or smoothies several times a week?
- ❑ Purchase magazines at newsstands when an annual subscription would be less expensive?
- ❑ Waste money on body piercing and tattoos? What's it going to look like thirty years from now?
- ❑ Buy clothes and wear them only once or never at all? (Yeah, yeah, yeah, the salesperson told you it looked really cute.)
- ❑ Buy a lot of gifts for your friends and family?
- ❑ Purchase only brand name, high-end items even though you know some generic or store brands are often just as good?
- ❑ Buy all the latest health and beauty aids even though you have un-opened or partially used products at home? Was it the new packaging that made you buy more?
- ❑ Add new DVDs to your collection because you've developed the habit of buying all the recent releases?
- ❑ Buy CD's and listen to them just once?
- ❑ Go to an evening movie when you could have easily gone to a matinee?
- ❑ Buy the latest electronic equipment as soon as it's released even though you know the prices will drop in a couple of months?
- ❑ Hold on to defective or poor fitting merchandise instead of returning it to the seller?
- ❑ Overbuy unnecessary clearance items because you think you're saving money?

- ❑ Eat your lunch out excessively when you know you could save money by making it at home?
- ❑ Loan money to friends and never get it back?
- ❑ Drain your budget with excessive and frequent fast food purchases?
- ❑ Buy cigarettes?
- ❑ Pay for features on your cell phone that you don't really need or use?
- ❑ Order pay-per-view movies and then fall asleep?
- ❑ Waste money on fashion accessories that you wear only once?
- ❑ Buy high-end, more expensive products at airports, movie theatres, hotel gift and specialty shops, etc?
- ❑ Often pay late charges on video and game rentals?

Is it possible you could be wasting $10, $50, $100 or even more a month on junk and other miscellaneous purchases?

Were you able to identify some of your spending leaks?

Can you find ways to spend less and save more?

Do you spend $5 on smoothies or "designer" coffee every day?
If you eliminated this purchase just twice a week you would save
$10 a week or $40 a month. That's $480.00 a year you could add to
your savings.

What about haircuts, manicures, pedicures, waxing, etc? Could you cut
back on the frequency with which you schedule these services?
If you eliminated just $18 a month from this category, you would save
$216 a year.

Americans in general are deeper in debt than ever. Bankruptcy filings
are at an all-time high, and personal savings are ridiculously low. This is
the result of poor financial habits. If you want to save more money and
improve your financial habits, then you must understand why and
where you spend your money. If you reduced your spending by just
$2.75 a day, you would have $1,004 within a year. If you invested
$1,004 at 10% a year, you would have $57,504 in just over 20 years!
Not bad, huh? What are you waiting for?

Keep high aspirations, moderate expectations, and small needs.

— *William Howard Stein*

CREDIT CARD MANAGEMENT

Money was invented so we could know exactly how much we owe.

— *Cullen Hightower*

You open your mail and discover you have just received a pre-approved credit card. The credit limit is high and the introductory rate is low. It's very appealing. What's the first thought that crosses your mind?

1. How fast can I get to the mall to buy the latest electronic gadget or outfit?

2. Wow, I've entered the big leagues. Let the spending begin!

3. Should I do some research to better understand the ins and outs of using a credit card?

In addition to question number three, you should also ask:

- If I choose to use the card, what are the financial consequences?

- Is there a grace period for the payment due date?

- What's all the small print on the back of the welcome letter?

- Will I pay only for what I purchase or will I have to pay interest too?

- Is there an annual fee for using the card?

- How do I manage my spending to make sure I don't get into debt?

- What if I don't want to use credit cards at all?

- Do I really need to establish a credit profile?

Without a credit history you could have a difficult time navigating through life on your own. When you're ready to get an apartment, property owners will check your credit history. If you don't have a credit history or if it's blemished, it is very likely you will be required to make a deposit prior to moving in or have someone co-sign for you. Without a credit history, many utility companies will require a deposit before turning on your electricity and other services. Additionally, any deposits you make will not be returned to you for at least a year.

Buying a car without a credit history will result in higher interest rates. Even getting car insurance will be more difficult because insurance companies demand a good credit record as well. You could even be turned down for a job because potential employers check your credit history too.

The **Rich Choices** in this chapter are divided into the following three sections: **Getting the Best Credit Card Deal, Using Your Card Responsibly,** and **What to Do If You're Already In Debt.**

 RICH CHOICES

Getting the Best Credit Card Deal

- Shop Around for the Best Rates
- Pay Attention to the Grace Period
- Understand the Terms and Costs
- Be Aware of Penalties
- Start Early

SHOP AROUND FOR THE BEST RATES

The most common and widely used form of credit is the credit card. A credit card is a form of borrowing that usually involves interest (or finance charges) on the amounts charged. Credit can be a friend or a foe, an asset or a liability.

Credit cards are issued through many different providers. Banks, credit unions, department stores, and other businesses all issue credit cards. Credit is not free and your costs will depend on:

- From whom you borrow

- Your credit history

- The agreed upon terms
- How much you charge
- Whether or not you carry a balance
- How long you take to pay off your balance

Major credit card companies spend a lot of time and money attracting customers because they want your business. Don't sign up for the first offer that appears in your mail box. Shop around. Spend some time studying the terms and costs before signing on the dotted line.

Some very basic cards have low-rates and no annual fees. Credit card companies offer a variety of different interest rates and annual fees. Check out www.bankrate.com. This site will help you compare offers from issuers around the country. Be sure to consider offers from local banks and credit unions. Get a card with a low interest rate. The lower the rate the less money you'll pay on unpaid balances.

PAY ATTENTION TO THE GRACE PERIOD

This is really important. The Grace Period is the period of time, usually 25 days, after you buy something during which interest is not charged. If you pay your bill in full and on time, you will not be charged interest. If, however, you pay the minimum (which I don't recommend), or make only a partial payment, interest will be added to your un-paid balance. Some credit card issuers are reducing the interest-free grace periods on credit cards from 25 days to 20 and still others have no grace periods at all. Having no grace period means interest is added to every purchase immediately. You want to avoid this at all costs.

UNDERSTAND THE TERMS AND COSTS

Before signing on the dotted line, be sure to read and understand the small print. Creditors can change the terms of the agreement with only 15 days notice. These notices come in the mail with your statement, and yes, the print is small. Read these notices carefully. If there's something you don't understand, call your credit card company and get clarification.

I know people who won't call because they don't want to appear stupid or unknowledgeable over the phone. Come on, telephone reps don't know you and besides, that's their job. Their primary responsibility is to assist you and to answer your questions. If you don't get a satisfactory explanation, hang up, call back, and speak with another representative. Don't worry about what they think. BE POLITE, BE ASSERTIVE! Do whatever it takes to get clarification.

BE AWARE OF PENALTIES

Again, read the fine print. The bold print giveth while the fine print taketh away. What happens if you miss a payment, make a late payment, or exceed your credit limit? Penalty rates and fees continually increase. Pay careful attention to the consequences of making a late payment.

START EARLY

Leaving high school or college and transitioning to the working world will be a lot tougher without a credit history. It will be even tougher if you decide to forgo college and head into the working world directly out of high school. No matter what, you need to establish your credit profile early on.

What about credit's initial "Catch 22?" You can't build up a credit history without a credit card, and it's really tough to get a credit card without a credit history. Right? Not really. While you're in high school or college you don't have to worry about this because credit card companies will be inundating you with offers. They're not too worried about you not paying because they know your parents will cover any shortage if you use the card and are unable to pay.

Experts agree: it is better to learn about proper credit card management while you're young and still living at home. It's a good idea to get a card with a very low credit limit. This will make it more difficult to get into financial trouble. You'll be better prepared when you enter college or the workplace because you'll have a good understanding of how to use your card wisely. Get a credit card and by all means, use it responsibly!

☀ RICH CHOICES ☀

Use Your Credit Card Responsibly

- Don't Spend What You Can't Repay
- Pay More Than the "Minimum Amount Due"
- Pay Attention to the Warning Signs
- Set a Credit Card Budget
- Avoid Cash Advances
- Check Your Statements Thoroughly Prior to Making Payments
- Don't Carry Too Many Credit Cards
- Don't Commingle Your Credit with Someone Who Has Bad Credit
- Don't Let Friends Use Your Credit Card
- Monitor Your Credit Report

DON'T SPEND WHAT YOU CAN'T REPAY

Sounds so obvious, doesn't it? Makes you wonder why so many adults end up in credit card debt, huh? Using a credit card is borrowing money and paying it back with interest. Because you're not using cash, it's important to keep track of what you've charged to your credit card. It's very easy to make purchases when all you have to do is pull out the "plastic." Easy that is, until the bill arrives. Shopping with a credit card is painless and easy, so easy that many of us forget what we've purchased. We don't realize how quickly the charges add up.

Charge only what you know you can pay back each month. Remember, if you use your card for everyday items, you will pay a very high premium, assuming you don't pay off your balance in full every month. A good rule to follow is this: If you don't have the cash to pay for an item, then you shouldn't be charging it to your credit card.

PAY MORE THAN THE "MINIMUM AMOUNT DUE"

Paying the minimum amount due is like treading water. Because of the magic of compounding, when you pay only the minimum amount you end up paying for a very long time. Here's an example: If your balance is $2,000, and your interest rate is 18 percent, and you made only minimum payments, it will take you almost 19 years to pay off your balance. Worse yet, you will pay $2,615 in interest charges alone. When you don't pay your balance in full each month your money is being wasted because of compound interest.

PAY ATTENTION TO THE WARNING SIGNS

You run the risk of ruining your financial future if you abuse your credit privileges or develop poor credit habits. If you can't pay off your balance in full each month, or if you are using one card to pay off another, stop charging right away. You're heading for trouble. Heed these warning signs and stop using the card!

SET A CREDIT CARD BUDGET

It's a good idea to limit your monthly credit spending to 10 percent of your monthly (after tax) income. For example, if you take home $500 a month, spend no more than $50 a month on credit.

AVOID CASH ADVANCES

Taking a cash advance on your credit card is borrowing money from your creditor. It's not a good idea and should be avoided at all costs. Getting a cash advance is really easy, too easy in fact. What you may not realize, however, is how much that trip to the ATM (Automatic Teller Machine) will end up costing.

The extra fees associated with cash advances are very high. Before taking a cash advance, ask yourself if it's really necessary. If you're using the money to pay a bill or to cover expenses until you receive your regular paycheck, then you're probably already in trouble. Here's the cash advance lowdown:

- Cash advances have a higher interest rate than regular card charges.

- You'll be charged an up-front fee of 2 to 4 percent of the amount of your cash advance.

- There is no grace period on cash advances. You will be charged interest immediately when you receive the cash from the ATM.

- Many card companies require you to pay off your regular credit card balance before you pay off the cash advance balance. This is because the interest on the cash advance amount is higher, which means they make money while you stay in debt longer.

CHECK YOUR STATEMENTS THOROUGHLY PRIOR TO MAKING PAYMENTS

When you receive your statements, take a few moments and verify all the charges are legitimate. Also, check to be sure you have received credit for disputed items or for items you may have returned to a seller. Checking your statements is also a precautionary measure to ensuring you're not a victim of credit card fraud.

DON'T CARRY TOO MANY CREDIT CARDS

Credit can give you a false sense of achievement. Carry just one or two cards for all your purchases. Limiting your accounts reduces paperwork and record keeping.

DON'T COMMINGLE YOUR CREDIT WITH SOMEONE WHO HAS BAD CREDIT

Don't cosign for your friends' automobiles, apartments, cell phones, etc. Your credit will be negatively affected because of late payments or no payments at all. If you feel deeply inclined to cosign, then say "yes" only after you have totally accepted the fact that you can afford to lose that amount of money. It is your responsibility to use your credit wisely.

DON'T LET FRIENDS USE YOUR CREDIT CARD

If a friend asks to use your card and promises to pay you back when the bill comes – don't do it. This is simply another way of asking for a loan that may not be repaid. Remember, it's your name on the card. It's up to you to manage it responsibly. You will discover in life most people will not have a problem saying "no" to your request! Have the courage to say "That is something I don't do! Sorry, I wish I could help." You will find two things when you say "No": (1) People will respect you, or (2) they will get mad at you. If they get mad…oh well!

MONITOR YOUR CREDIT REPORT

Credit Bureaus monitor your spending habits and your payment history. Your credit report documents whether you pay your bills on time, in full, or whether you pay just the minimum amount due. A bad rating and a "slow pay" record will affect your ability to borrow in the future for big things like a car, a house, and your college education!

Having good credit can help you get additional credit and may help you to get credit at a better rate. Review your credit report and check it for inaccuracies. Yes, the three major credit bureaus do make mistakes and it's your responsibility to know what's on your report. Check it for incorrect balances or for accounts you may not have opened, which could indicate an identity theft problem. If errors appear, you have the right and the responsibility to provide a written statement to make the correction. The credit bureaus will investigate and in certain instances, they will remove the item from your report.

THE CREDIT BUREAUS:

Equifax
To order report: 1-800-685-1111 / 800-505-2136
To report fraud: 1-800-525-6285 - Web site: equifax.com

Experian (formerly TRW)
To order report: 1-888-397-3742 / 800-301-7195
To report fraud: 1-888-397-3742 - Web site: experian.com

TransUnion LLC
To order report: 1-800-888-4213 / 800-680-7289
To report fraud: 1-800-916-8800 - Web site: transunion.com

☀ RICH CHOICES ☀

What To Do If You're Already in Debt

- Get Real
- Immediately Contact Your Creditors, Don't Hide From Them
- Negotiate with Creditors
- Stop Using the Card and Start Using Cash
- Prioritize Your Debt
- Consider Balance Transfers
- Pay More Than the "Minimum Amount Due"
- Keep Your Word
- Make Regular, On-Time Payments
- Establish Voluntary Credit Limits
- Secure It

Get Real

If you're unable to pay your bills and your debts are mounting, you need a plan and you need it fast. You can get out of debt. It won't be quick or easy, but it can be done. You've got to face it to erase it!

Immediately Contact Your Creditors, Don't Hide From Them

Creditors must know of your problems before your payments are overdue. Many creditors will work with you to make alternative arrangements. Working with creditors may help you to avoid having your account sent to an independent collection agency. Accounts sent to collections are reported to the credit bureaus. This negatively impacts your credit profile. Inform creditors as to how you intend to make payments. Don't hide from the situation you've created, deal with it.

Negotiate with Creditors

Pick up the phone and call your credit card company. Say something like, "I realize I owe $250 this month. I can only pay $100. Can you help me eliminate the late fee and the interest charges this month?" This technique works very well. You have nothing to lose by giving it a try.

Stop Using the Card and Start Using Cash

If you can't make full credit card payments, use cash until you are able to effectively manage a budget, monitor your spending, and eliminate excessive purchases. Do not use any more credit. Eliminate temptations to use the card by hiding it, cutting it up, or giving it to someone you trust to hold for you. There is an expression that is so wise: "Money comes and money goes, but your money should not always be waving good bye!"

PRIORITIZE YOUR DEBT

Total up all your debt. Write down the names of your creditors. List how much you owe each one and what the interest rates are. This will help you to see where you are. Pay off the cards with the highest interest rates first. Of course, you must still make regular, on-time payments to your other creditors.

CONSIDER BALANCE TRANSFERS

If your credit card debt is spread out across many accounts, consider balance transfers. Balance transfers occur when you transfer your higher interest balances to another credit card with a lower interest rate. Some issuers charge a fee for transferring a balance. Be sure to shop around to avoid excessive transfer fees. Once you've completed the transfer, continue to make payments to your old card while you're waiting for your new one. This way you won't be charged late fees by your old credit card company. Finally, find out if the transfer rate is just for transferred balances or for new purchases only.

PAY MORE THAN THE "MINIMUM AMOUNT DUE"

The "Minimum Amount Due" on a credit card is calculated as a percentage of your current balance. Interest keeps piling up and your money gets sucked into a compound interest sinkhole. Pay as much as you can every month to avoid paying more in interest charges.

KEEP YOUR WORD

If creditors agree to work with you, be sure to follow through according to your agreements. Commit to a payment plan that is realistic and reasonable. Don't give up.

MAKE REGULAR, ON-TIME PAYMENTS

Paying late or not paying at all will only make the situation worse. Late payments not only blemish your credit score, they can also result in higher interest rates and make it difficult for you to negotiate better interest rates in the future.

ESTABLISH VOLUNTARY CREDIT LIMITS

Have your creditor lower your credit limit. If the card is for emergencies only, you don't need thousands of credit dollars available to tempt you.

SECURE IT

A secured credit card is obtained by depositing money into an account as collateral. In exchange for your deposit, you'll receive a credit card for the exact amount you deposited. Oftentimes, individuals obtain a secured card to help establish their payment history. This is the means I used to help restore my bad credit.

Be sure to get a secured card from a major, reputable bank. Stick to smaller purchases so you can pay off your balance in full each month and avoid interest charges. Shop around for the best offers. Look for a card that charges no application or processing fees. Additionally, make sure the annual fees and interest rates are low. Again, www.Bankrate.com is a great resource. They list secured card offers from banks around the country.

Action may not always bring happiness; but there is no happiness without action.

— *Benjamin Disraeli*

A LAURIE'S STORY

The Credit Card Blues!

Children have never been very good at listening to their elders, but they have never failed to imitate them.

—James Baldwin

I received my first credit card while in college and I took full advantage of all of its privileges. I started spending right away. I knew the card was supposed to be used for emergencies and necessary items. However, my definition of "necessary" and "emergency" was pizza for me and my friends. Being the one with the credit card made me feel important and valued.

Using the card felt like free money. I was acting "as if" I had money when I didn't. Having one credit card made me feel so good, I applied for others. Looking back, spending money I didn't have gave me a false sense of accomplishment. I had credit without the skills to manage it effectively and without the resources to meet my financial obligations.

I loved being able to use my credit card for everything. The best part was opening my bill and seeing that the minimum payment due was only $15. I thought it was wonderful that I could pay only $15. I kept thinking, "I'll catch up next month and pay off the entire balance then." I didn't realize how quickly interest charges and late fees were adding up. Making minimum payments, incurring late charges, and continuing to spend excessively got me into a whole lot of trouble.

By the time I realized my balances were out of control, it was too late. I had incurred over one thousand dollars in late charges, penalties, and interest charges. I made my situation worse by acting "as if" everything was fine. I didn't want to face my responsibilities. I tried to run from my problems by ignoring them. In my attempt to avoid creditors, I stopped answering the phone and I stopped opening my mail. I was hoping the problem would just go away. I felt powerless and ashamed. I didn't realize the credit bureaus were tracking my negative payment history. Eventually, all my negligence caught up with me.

By the time I graduated from college, I could not rent a car, buy a car, lease an apartment, or get a phone in my name. The information on my credit report indicated I was a risk to any potential creditor. As a result, I had to pay extra for everything. In addition to paying higher rates, I was also required to make advance deposits for services. I qualified for nothing. I was humiliated and ashamed. All my past activities were on my credit reports and there was no way to hide from them. Being in debt was debilitating. I hadn't realized how much my earlier spending sprees would affect my future. It took me several years to get my financial life back on track.

How I Became Debt Free – While I was paying off my credit card debt, I was working to develop better spending habits. When considering a credit card purchase I would immediately ask myself two questions: "If I don't have the money to pay for this in cash today, what makes me think I'll have the money in 30 days?" and "Do I need it or do I want it?" These two questions helped me to get a handle on my spending. I learned to delay gratification and to sacrifice. I also became more self-disciplined. I stopped acting "as if" I was wealthy!

When you're turned down for credit, you have the right to receive a free copy of your credit report. Needless to say, I had quite a few opportunities to view my reports. When I finally paid off my credit card debts, my credit rating was dismally low. As a result I was unable to get another credit card for years.

Initially I considered applying for department store or gas cards to help re-build my credit. I did some research and learned that these cards came with high interest rates and low credit limits. Additionally, some issuers of department store cards did not report to the credit bureaus. Here I was trying to re-establish my credit worthiness and I wasn't going to have proof of my timely payments. Having an unreported card account was not going to help boost my credit one bit. If they weren't reporting it to the credit bureaus, it didn't do me any good.

I found the solution in a secured credit card. A secured credit card looks and works much like any other credit card. It's "secured" because the cardholder is required to make a deposit to the creditor first. I deposited $500 and I had a credit card with a $500 limit. My deposit guaranteed the card issuer that the bill would be paid. If I didn't make payments, the creditor didn't care, they already had my money.

I kept my purchases to a minimum to ensure I could pay the balance in full each month. After a year of on-time payments with a secured card

I applied for, and received, an unsecured credit card with a lower interest rate. When I closed the secured credit card account, my $500 deposit was returned to me. Getting a secured credit card helped me to re-establish my credit.

Today I use just one card for all my purchases. Getting out of debt required a lot of hard work and self-discipline. It didn't happen overnight, but it did happen over a substantial period of time! As embarrassing as it is for me to admit to this huge mistake, I am sharing it with you in hopes that you will learn from my bad experience. If you, dear reader, will be spared the bitter lesson I had to learn, all my pain will have been worth it!

Remember, credit cards managed responsibly can put you on the road towards establishing a respectable credit profile. Misused, they can ruin your credit profile and cost you a lot of time, money, and heartache. As always… it's your cash, your credit, your choice!

However long the night, the dawn will break.

— *African Proverb*

Activity

Are You Credit Worthy? The Credit Card Quiz!

Check Your Understanding of Credit by Answering True or False to the Following Questions:

1. Taking out a cash advance using your credit card is the same as making a purchase with the card.
   True   False
   Cash advances have a higher interest rate than regular card charges. Additionally, there is no grace period on cash advances. You will be charged interest immediately when you receive the cash from the ATM.

2. The payment due date is always one month from when you receive your credit card statement.
   True   False
   Payment due dates and grace periods vary by credit cards. Be sure you know what it is.

3. Creditors look at income, expenses, and other characteristics to determine if you're a good candidate for credit.
   True   False
   Creditors look at many characteristics of the applicant to determine if they should extend credit to them. They check with the credit bureaus to find out your repayment history and your credit score. A good credit profile is one that indicates a history of prompt and reliable payments.

4. A grace period lets you avoid finance charges if you pay your balance in full before the due date.
   True   False
   Paying your balance in full before the due date means you will not pay any finance or interest charges.

5. Credit reports are available only to creditors and other people.
   True   False
   You can obtain a copy of your credit report for free (if you were recently denied credit, are unemployed, or a victim of fraud) or for a fee by writing to any of the three credit bureaus. You can also check out freecreditreport.com for additional information.

6. Late payments don't show up on your credit report.
   True   False
   Whenever you are more than 30 days late, it will be reported to the credit bureau.

7. You will not be penalized if you pay less than the minimum payment.
   True   False
   You must send in the minimum amount required by the due date or the creditor may consider your payment late and charge additional fees. This will also be reported to the credit bureau. It's best to pay your bill in full each month.

8. Bad information is erased from you credit report once the debt is paid in full.
   True   False
   Credit reports will continue to list bad information for seven years, ouch!

9. Credit bureaus will investigate each item on your report if you write a letter disputing the item.
   True   False
   If an item is more trouble than it's worth, the credit bureau will simply remove it from your report rather than investigate it. It worked for me!

10. If something is incorrect on your report, you have no recourse; there is nothing you can do about it.
    True   False
    If something is incorrect or the creditor who provided the information cannot verify it, the credit bureau must remove it from your report.

11. Creditors want to know you pay your monthly bills consistently on time.
    True   False
    Knowing you pay your bills on time lets them know that you're reliable. Creditors want to loan money to people they believe will repay debt.

Never spend your money before you have earned it.

— Thomas Jefferson

1–False, 2–False, 3–True, 4–True, 5–False, 6–False, 7–False, 8–False, 9–False, 10–False, 11–True

Checking Accounts

Until you are happy with who you are, you will never be happy with what you have.

— Zig Zigler

Checking accounts are safe and convenient. They provide you with a way to make deposits, cash checks, and easily access your money.

The checking account is:

- A **FINANCIAL** tool – a way for you to manage your money.

- NOT a **FINANCING** tool – can't access money that's not yours.

Opening a checking account is simple and easy. When you open one you will be given a debit card and you will purchase checks. Blank checks allow you to take your money out of the bank when necessary. The debit card looks like a credit card and operates in much the same way. Debit cards provide you with access to your money via ATM's. These two items, the debit card and the checkbook, allow you to handle most of your banking needs.

☀ RICH CHOICES ☀

Developing Good Checking Account Habits

- Balance Your Checkbook and Reconcile Your Statements Regularly
- Avoid ATM Charges
- Avoid Account Service Fees
- Use Duplicate Checks
- Use a Pen When Writing Checks and Don't Erase Your Mistakes
- Never Sign a Blank Check
- Don't Write Checks Against Money You Don't Have
- Use Direct Deposit
- Use Overdraft Protection

Balance Your Checkbook and Reconcile Your Statements Regularly

Develop the habit of reviewing your bank statement every single month so you know exactly how much money you have. Record every transaction and keep track of when you use your debit card, the ATM, or make withdrawals and deposits. Compare your statement against your check register. You can also access your account via telephone or online to get the most up-to-date information about your account. Without this knowledge, you run the risk of bouncing checks.

A debit card is like having an ATM card that writes checks for you. Like checks, debit cards can be used to pay for things you purchase. You have to keep track of ATM slips and debit card receipts. Withdrawals add up very quickly. Calculate your balance after every transaction to eliminate the risk of overdrawing your account. It takes only a few minutes and it helps you avoid overdrafts and other service fees.

Avoid ATM Charges

When you use the ATM of your bank, you will not pay a fee. Use the ATM of banks you don't have an account with and you will be charged a fee. I know people who pay monthly ATM fees in excess of $20.00; that's $240 a year to access their own money! Planning ahead and being proactive can solve this problem. Don't wait until the last minute to think about your cash requirements. Plan ahead and go to your own bank to get cash.

Avoid Account Service Fees

Don't be caught off guard. Find out when you open an account what the fees are. Understand how your bank processes checks. Some banks may process the largest checks first. If you don't have enough money in your account to cover the largest check, all subsequent checks processed that day will bounce. Each time this happens you will be hit with a separate charge.

Avoid the monthly minimum balance fee as well. Many checking accounts require you to maintain a minimum balance. If your balance falls below this amount, you will be charged a monthly fee. Try to maintain the minimum balance and avoid these fees.

Use Duplicate Checks

If you think you may forget to record all your transactions, get a checkbook with duplicate checks. Each check you write has its own carbon copy. By creating this simultaneous record, you will always know to whom and for how much you wrote each check. No guessing and no surprises.

Use a Pen When Writing Checks and Don't Erase Your Mistakes

If you make an error when writing a check, write "Void" across the check and then tear or shred it. In some cases you can make the correction and place your initials next to the mistake. I recommend starting over with a new check.

Never Sign a Blank Check

Checks are a form of money. Fill in the payee and the amount line completely on all your checks. Don't leave blank spaces that can be altered. Write the check amount as far to the left as you can. This way changes to the amount cannot be made by someone else. Don't use other people's checks or let them use yours. Keep your checks and other documents containing your private information in a safe place.

Don't Write Checks Against Money You Don't Have

It's illegal and it's stupid to write a check when you know you don't have the money in your account to cover the amount. The charge for bouncing a check can run as high as $25 or $30 each. In addition, you probably will be charged a fee by the vendor. Many times, before you can get to the bank and make a deposit large enough to stop the "hemorrhaging" you will have accumulated a total of a few hundred dollars in fees! What a painful lesson!

USE DIRECT DEPOSIT

Direct Deposit is smart and efficient. Many employers allow employees to set up Direct Deposit. This means your check is directly deposited into your account. Having your money electronically deposited saves you time and money, and is a more efficient way for you to manage your finances. It saves time because you don't have to make trips to the bank. It also eliminates the possibility of your check being lost in the mail, misplaced, or stolen. Many banks will even reduce or waive their fees if you use Direct Deposit.

USE OVERDRAFT PROTECTION

If for some reason you do make an error and write a check for more than you have in your account, there are ways to protect yourself. The least expensive way is to link your checking account to your savings account. Should you not have the money in your checking account, the funds from your savings account will transfer into your checking. This is to cover the amount of the overdraft. Other options include establishing a Line of Credit with your bank or to have the overdraft amounts charged to your credit card. Both these options are more expensive and have high interest rates associated with them. Bottom line: Know how much you have in your checking account at all times!

> *Work joyfully and peacefully, knowing that right thoughts and right efforts inevitably bring about right results.*
>
> —*James Allen*

A LAURIE STORY

Everything CHECKS Out – Almost!

The unexamined life is not worth living.

— *Socrates*

I pay all my bills through on-line banking. I find this to be simple, convenient and efficient. I've even set up a couple of my on-going, consistent payments on automatic bill pay. Regarding my checking account, I'm happy to report that everything *checks* out.

Ok, ok – I do have one, two confessions to make. I don't balance my checkbook, and for a long time my Social Security number was my checking account number. Ok, I've said it. Now I must do something about it. I recently had my checking account number changed. I haven't, however, found a balancing system that works for me long-term. I've asked many people about their balancing techniques, and I've tried a few. Over the past year I've experimented with several methods, but I don't stick with any of them. After about three months, I just stop. Could it be that I'm just not committed? Oh, please, say it's not true. I can't stand it. I feel like I'm committed, and I tell myself I'm going to do better.

Now, let me make a couple of things clear. I do spend a few minutes each month ensuring my deposits are reflected in my account, and I monitor all transactions and compare them against my account statement. I compare my on-line account statements with the hand-written entries from my ledger at the end of each month. I just don't go through the process of balancing to the penny.

I've decided to make this one of my short-term goals. I will no longer make excuses about this issue. I've put it off long enough. I'm going to use the balancing ledger instructions included in the activity section of this chapter.

> *Money will buy you a bed, but not a good night's sleep, a house but not a home, a companion but not a friend.*
>
> — *Zig Ziglar*

Activity

The Balancing Act!

One of the responsibilities of owning a checking account is keeping it up-to-date. This includes recording all transactions, keeping a running balance in your checkbook, and reconciling your checkbook balance with the banks checking account statement each month.

Balance or reconcile your checking account with the following steps:

1. When you receive your bank statement, compare your monthly bank statement against entries written in your checkbook (check register). Put a check mark next to each item on the statement as you find the check, ATM, or debit card entry in your register.

2. Record any ATM fees, returned check fees, or service fees that you may not have recorded.

3. Record automatic on-line bill payments for consistent monthly items like insurance, cable, car payments, etc.

4. Add automatic deposits for direct deposit items.

5. Add any interest you may have earned.

6. Check your bank statement for outstanding items. These are the things not yet checked off on your statement. Total the outstanding transactions.

7. Subtract the outstanding transaction total from the ending balance on your bank statement. This is your new balance.

8. Add any recent deposits not yet reflected on your bank statement to your new balance. This number should match your checkbook ending balance. If not, repeat steps one through eight making sure you recorded all deposits, withdrawals, and ATM transactions. Check your math and make sure you did not transpose any numbers.

> *Time and money spent in helping men to do more for themselves is far better than mere giving.*
>
> — *Henry Ford*

TIME IS MONEY

You can't turn back the clock, but you can wind it up again.

— *Bonnie Prudden*

When Benjamin Franklin said "Time is money," he was warning us against the squandering of time. He continued by saying "for that is the stuff that life is made of." Following are three simple financial success tools based on the foundation of time. Understanding these financial concepts along with an understanding of general investment principles will help you achieve your financial goals.

RICH CHOICES

Time is Money

- Compounding
- Rule of 72
- Dollar Cost Averaging

COMPOUNDING

Time is your greatest asset if you are a young investor. The younger you are when you start investing, the more you will benefit from compounding. Compounding is a phenomenal financial concept where time works in your favor. Compounding occurs when your investment earns money and that money is then added to your principal, your initial investment. This forms a larger base on which earning may accumulate.

As your investment base gets larger, it has the potential to grow faster than it would with simple interest. With simple interest, your investment earns money only on the principal. Thanks to compounding, if you saved only $2,000 a year for 10 years, earning 10 percent a year, you would have $506,000 by age 65. You see, time really is money.

When you save and invest, you make money by earning interest. The interest may be calculated in two ways:

- **SIMPLE INTEREST** – Interest is calculated on your principal only. In other words, interest is earned only on the money you put in, your deposits.

- **COMPOUND INTEREST** – Interest you earn on the investment also earns interest. That's interest added to interest you've already earned.

As the following example shows, if you had $5,000 in an account that paid 5 percent annually in simple interest for five years, you'd earn $250 a year, for a total of $1,250 in interest. The same $5,000 investment paying 5 percent interest compounded annually for five years would produce a total of $1,381.41 in interest. That's $131.41 more than you would earn from simple interest.

Compound Interest vs. Simple Interest		
$5,000 invested at 5% (annual) Interest		
	Compound	Simple
Start	$5,000.00	$5,000.00
After 1 year	$5,250.00	$5,250.00
After 2 years	$5,512.50	$5,500.00
After 3 years	$5,788.13	$5,750.00
After 4 years	$6,077.53	$6,000.00
After 5 years	$6,381.41	$6,250.00
Growth	27.6%	25%

RULE OF 72

The Rule of 72 is a very important financial success tool. According to this rule you can calculate how long it will take for your savings or investments to double. You can do this by dividing the interest rate into 72. Here are two examples:

1. Money earning 6% interest would take 12 years to double. $72 \div 6 = 12$

2. Money earning 12% interest would take 6 years to double. $72 \div 12 = 6$

DOLLAR COST AVERAGING

If you can count on nothing else, count on this: the stock market will go up and it will go down. What you can't predict is when. For many people, that uncertainty can make investing difficult. Fortunately, there are effective strategies to put the odds in your favor and put more money in your pocket. One such strategy is called dollar cost averaging.

The concept of dollar cost averaging goes something like this: you invest the same amount of money in an investment every month regardless of whether the price is going up or going down. When you dollar cost average, you invest a specific amount of money at regular intervals. Dollar cost averaging helps you reduce your investment risk. It lessens the risk of investing a large amount of money in one investment at the wrong time. This is because your money buys more shares when prices are low and fewer shares when prices are high.

Since there are no guarantees in stock or mutual fund investments, and we can't predict what the market will do, dollar cost averaging takes the guesswork out of the process. This strategy is not a guarantee of investment success. You still have to make wise choices about which stocks or mutual funds to buy.

When it comes to saving and investing, time really is money, especially for the early investor. It's safe to say that the longer you invest your money, the more you'll have when you need it. Strategies like compounding, rule of 72, and dollar cost averaging are critical to creating financial success. Take advantage of them when you begin earning and investing money.

Concentrate all your thoughts upon the work at hand. The sun's rays do not burn until brought to a focus.

— Alexander Graham

A LAURIE STORY

Penny Power!

The whole secret to a successful life is to find out what it is your destiny to do, and then do it.

— *Henry Ford*

When I was in high school a math teacher presented our class with the following hypothetical scenario: We had just won a contest. We had to choose between two grand prizes and we only had thirty seconds to make our decision. Here were our options:

- **Option One** – $1,000 per day for 30 days.

- **Option Two** – A penny the first day, two pennies the second day, four pennies the third day, and so on. Each day's pay is double the pay from the previous day for 30 days.

Which would you choose? More than half the students simply chose option one because it was immediately obvious we could walk away with $30,000. Most of us didn't bother to calculate the second option. We chose instead to spend the remainder of our thirty seconds fantasizing about how we were going to spend our money.

A few students assumed there must be some sort of trick and without really knowing why, chose option two. There was one girl who used her thirty seconds to put pen to paper. By the time she reached day twenty-two she calculated she would have $20,971 by choosing the pennies.

The students sat there dumfounded as the calculations were put on the chalkboard. Through the power of compound interest, we would have $10,737,418 by choosing option two. Wow, almost 11 million dollars!!!

DAY	AMOUNT OF PENNIES
1	1
2	2
3	4
4	8
5	16
6	32
7	64
8	128
9	256
10	512
11	1024
12	2048
13	4096
14	8192
15	16384
16	32768
17	65536
18	131072
19	262144
20	524288
21	1048576
22	2097152
23	4194304
24	8388608
25	16777216
26	33554432
27	67108864
28	134217728
29	268435456
30	536870912
31	$ 10,737,418.24

This exercise taught me to respect and value small amounts of money. I also learned there are no shortcuts in life. My laziness and unwillingness to do the calculations cost me. Sitting in the back of the room laughing with my friends got me nowhere. This is exactly how it is in life too!

To create financial wealth you must commit to consistently making positive, well-informed rich choices. Decide what you want and then commit to creating the financial future you deserve. Understanding and taking advantage of the financial concepts and strategies covered in this chapter are essential to creating financial wealth. There's an expression:

"Watch the pennies and the dollars will take care of themselves." Do you respect and value small amounts of money?

> *Pennies do not come from heaven. They have to be earned here on earth.*
>
> — *Margaret Thatcher*

Activity

Strategizing!

If you invest $50 a month into a mutual fund, and the fund trades for $5 per share this month, you would be able to buy 10 shares (50 ÷ 5 = 10). Next month, if the mutual fund costs $8 per share, you would be able to buy 6 shares (50 ÷ 8 = 6.25). Because you invested this way, you own 16 shares and have reduced your risk because you paid, on average, $6.50 per share. What type of investment strategy does this represent?

1. Compounding

2. Rule of 72

3. Dollar Cost Averaging

Can you come up with your own idea of an investment strategy? Write it down.

_____

_____

_____

_____

_____

_____

_____

_____

Poverty is a great enemy to human happiness.

— *Samuel Johnson*

The correct answer is 3, Dollar Cost Averaging.

THE BIG PAYBACK –
INVESTING 101

You're going to have to find out where you want to go. And then you've got to start going there. But immediately. You can't afford to lose a minute.

—*J. D. Salinger*

When it comes to investing, the advantage is always given to the early investor. Now is the time to start investing and taking advantage of all the opportunities that youth affords you! You see, time really is money. The earlier you start investing the better off you'll be.

One of the best ways to make your money grow is to invest in mutual funds. Mutual funds are a great way to meet your financial goals and buying mutual funds may be the smartest financial decision of your life. Considering today's high costs of living, and low interest rates on savings accounts, it makes sense to understand the basics of mutual fund investing. Mutual funds, once you understand how they work, can open up a whole new world of money-making opportunities for you.

WHAT IS A MUTUAL FUND? A mutual fund is a collection of stocks and or bonds. A mutual fund company specializes in handling groups of funds (stocks) from different corporations and organizations. The company then brings together groups of clients and invests their money. Each investor, that's you, owns a piece of the fund invested in multiple companies. Each of these pieces is referred to as a share and each share has a price tag.

Mutual Funds are a convenient and low-cost way to make money from stocks and bonds. It's easy because you don't have to buy the stocks directly. If a fund sells for $10 a share and you invest $100, you're the proud owner of 10 shares of the fund! Part of your $100 may have bought you stock in a telecommunications company. Some of your money may purchase shares of a clothing manufacturer, and another portion towards the purchase of an electronics company, etc. Your fund manager is responsible for selecting which companies to include in the mutual fund. They move stocks in and out of the fund to profit you.

☀ **RICH CHOICES** ☀

The Big Payback – Investing 101

- Know the Fundamentals of Mutual Funds
  1. It's Simple
  2. It's Diversified
  3. It's Easy to Get Started
  4. It's Affordable
  5. It's Yours
- Become a Lifelong Investor
- Don't Try to Make Quick Profits
- Know Thyself
- Read the Prospectus
- Make Your Money Work for You, Not for Your Stock Broker
- Stay the Course and Don't Give Up
- Mix It Up – Diversify, Diversify, Diversify
- Be Consistent and Persistent
- Act Now

KNOW THE FUNDAMENTALS OF MUTUAL FUNDS

1. It's Simple

If you were to buy and sell individual stocks or bonds on your own, it could be complicated, expensive, and time consuming. Mutual funds simplify the investment process by providing you, the investor, with a ready-made professionally managed fund at a reasonable price.

2. It's Diversified

Chances are you've heard the expression, *"Don't put all your eggs into one basket."* One of the key reasons for investing in mutual funds is they provide diversification. Because the funds are diversified, their values should not fluctuate as much as the price of an individual stock. Mutual funds help to minimize risk because your money is spread across many different investments. There are thousands of mutual funds from which to choose and each has its own strategy for making money. It's up to you to select the fund that best meets your individual needs.

3. It's Easy to Get Started

Opening a mutual fund is easy! In fact, the steps required to get started are just as easy as the steps required to open a checking account. Most banks have their own line of mutual funds, and the minimum investments are small. You can also open an account on-line.

4. It's Affordable

Sure, you can start with $25! Don't let the amount of your initial investment be your excuse not to get started, let it be your starting point. You don't have to have a lot of money to start investing in a mutual fund. In fact, some discount brokerage companies require financial commitments as low as $25-$50 a month. You must invest at least the minimum each month and, if you prefer, the monthly minimum can be deducted directly from your checking or savings account. Don't convince yourself that you can't invest because you don't have enough money to get started. Monitor and control your spending, and I'm sure you can easily come up with $25 a month. Start investing now. Stop making excuses, and start making money!

5. It's Yours

Yes, yes, yes! You can withdraw your money at any time by phone, by mail, or on-line.

BECOME A LIFELONG INVESTOR

Everyone, no matter what their age or financial status, should invest.

First, set aside enough cash for at least four to six months' of living expenses. This is an emergency fund that will be available in the event of illness or a period of unemployment. Then begin to invest. Invest in stocks either individually or in mutual funds, for long-term growth.

Develop the habit of investing regularly and systematically. Before you have the chance to spend all your money, pay yourself first. If you lack the discipline to make regular contributions, have your money automatically withdrawn from your checking or savings account. Commit yourself to regular and systematic investing now so you will have a foundation of money later.

Don't Try to Make Quick Profits

Investing is not a game. Don't try to make quick profits. If you are a young investor, time is on your side so invest for the long-term. The earlier you start investing, the more your investment base will grow. Don't focus too much on returns. Look at the long-term track record of the mutual fund and compare it to comparable funds.

Know Thyself

Don't take unnecessary risks with your money. Assess your emotions as an investor. Be sure you know your tolerance for risk and your investment objectives. Choose investments you are comfortable with and that you understand.

Read the Prospectus

Before investing in anything, read the prospectus carefully. Mutual funds and other investments are subject to strict federal regulations. Companies are required to give you a prospectus before you invest. The prospectus is an important document that spells out the objectives, fees, and risks associated with the investment. It contains a lot of valuable information. Never put your money into something that you do not fully understand.

MAKE YOUR MONEY WORK FOR YOU, NOT FOR YOUR STOCK BROKER

When it comes to commissions or fees on mutual funds, keep this simple rule in mind: don't pay any. Don't pay up front fees (charged when you invest in the fund) or back-end fees (when you withdraw from the fund). Some of these fees are called "loads" or "12b-fees." "Loads" are fees or sales charges that are paid to a salesperson for selling you the mutual fund. If you invest $25 into a mutual fund make sure the entire amount goes towards your investment. When you buy a "load" fund you miss out on the opportunity to invest all of your money. Over time, these fees can negatively impact the performance of your portfolio. When you invest in a "no-load" fund, all your money goes to work for you. Minimize your investment expenses by asking for "no-load" funds.

STAY THE COURSE AND DON'T GIVE UP

There are lots of different categories of funds and they all have different goals. Don't get discouraged if during your research you don't fully understand everything right away. Keep at it, ask questions, and educate yourself. Read, read, read some more. Review your portfolio at least once a year. When things in your life change, you may need to make changes to re-balance your portfolio to stay consistent with your long-term financial goals.

MIX IT UP – DIVERSIFY, DIVERSIFY, DIVERSIFY

Reduce your risks by investing in a broad range of investments. Building a diversified portfolio helps to spread your risk over a variety of investments. This may help you to achieve more consistent and desirable outcomes.

BE CONSISTENT AND PERSISTENT

Budget your money so you can continually add to your investments every month. Over time, your initial investment of $25 will turn into thousands. The two keys to growing wealth are consistency and persistence. Make your money work for you throughout your life.

ACT NOW

Procrastination robs you of your future. Every day you procrastinate will make reaching your goals more difficult. A basis rule of thumb is this: For every five years you wait to start investing, you may need to double your monthly investment amount to reach the same goal. Remember, it's not important how much you have to get started, it's that you GET started!

> *If you put off everything until you're sure of it, you'll get nothing done.*
>
> — *Norman Vincent Peale*

A LAURIE STORY

Wake Up and Mix It Up!

> *Vitality shows in not only the ability to persist but the ability to start over.*
>
> — *Francis Scott Key Fitzgerald*

I had invested a large portion of my savings in the individual stock of one company. When the company began to have financial trouble, I did nothing. I had been holding the stock for several years and it had performed very well. I became emotionally attached to the stock, and to the company. When I finally did wake up and pay attention, it was too late. The company began its filings for Chapter 11 bankruptcy and I lost almost $300,000! Yes, I know, I know. I was in shock, too. It hurt!

I took responsibility for my inaction and moved on. **Lesson: Pay attention and diversify YOUR INVESTMENTS.** If my holdings had been diversified, my losses would have been minimized. Once more, dear reader, please take heed of my mistake and do not repeat! Learn to cut your losses early. A u-turn is better than no turn. A good rule to follow is this: if you're holding an investment that you wouldn't buy today, then sell it and put whatever money you have left to work for you in another investment.

I always tried to turn every disaster into an opportunity.

— *John Davidson Rockefeller, Sr.*

Activity

Ten Years from Now...

List three of your financial goals.

GOALS

1. _____

2. _____

3. _____

What actions do you need to take to achieve them?

ACTION

1. _____

2. _____

3. _____

What is your time frame?

TIME FRAME

1. _____

2. _____

3. _____

I finally know what distinguishes man from the other beasts: financial worries.

—Jules Renard

THE ROTH IRA

The most pathetic person in the world is someone who has sight but no vision.

— Helen Keller

T he Roth IRA (Individual Retirement Account) is a terrific investment for anyone who qualifies. It provides a way for Americans to save money while benefiting from tax-free growth. It was established in 1998 and is named after former Senator William V. Roth, Jr.

- No, you're not too young for a Roth IRA.

- Yes, I realize you may be nine years old.

- Yes, it's that good!

☀ RICH CHOICES ☀

The Roth IRA

- Capitalize on the Advantages of a Roth IRA
  1. Withdraw Your Money Tax Free
  2. Withdraw Your Money and Your Earnings Without Penalty
  3. If You Earn Money You Can Open a Roth IRA
  4. It's Affordable
  5. It's Easy to Start
- Know the Difference Between a Roth IRA and a Traditional IRA
- Read the Small Print and Avoid Fees
- Be Consistent and Persistent
- Become a Lifelong Investor
- Act Now

Capitalize on the Advantages of a Roth IRA

1. Withdraw Your Money Tax Free

Besides fostering tax-free growth, the Roth IRA has flexible withdrawal rules. With a Roth IRA, you can withdraw any money you've put in, providing it's been in the account for at least five years. The only money that must remain in the account is the earnings. You don't pay taxes on the withdrawal because the money was taxed before you put it into the account.

2. Withdraw Your Money and Your Earnings Without Penalty

You can withdraw both your contribution and your earnings at any time, regardless of your age, provided the money is used for college or graduate school. You can also use up to $10,000 for a down payment on a first home. After you reach age $59^1/2$ (and you've had the account for at least five years), you can withdraw your earnings tax free and penalty free.

3. If You Earn Money You Can Open a Roth IRA

Money invested in a Roth IRA must be earned by you. It can't be money you received as a gift from your parents or money you've earned from other investments. If you're old enough to work and to earn money then you qualify for a Roth IRA. Money from odd jobs such as baby-sitting, pet-sitting, car washing, working around the house, and working at your parent's office all qualify as earnings. Keep in mind you may need a parent or guardian to co-sign on the account for you. Here are the maximum annual amounts you can contribute to a Roth IRA if you're under the age of 50: $3,000 in 2004, $4,000 in the years 2005 to 2007, and $5,000 in 2008.

4. It's Affordable

If you have earned income, you can't afford not to open a Roth IRA. Even just $10 a week or a month is better than nothing. It's ok to start small. Making regular contributions is a great way for you to develop the habit of saving and investing money.

5. It's Easy to Start

Opening a Roth IRA can be as simple as walking into a bank or brokerage firm and filling out a few forms and making a deposit. You can also set up a Roth IRA over the internet.

KNOW THE DIFFERENCE BETWEEN A ROTH IRA AND A TRADITIONAL IRA

- A Traditional IRA is a GOOD way to save for retirement.

- A Roth IRA is an EXCELLENT way to save for retirement.

Money contributed to a **Traditional IRA is Tax Deferred.** These are pre-tax dollars. This means you **DO NOT** pay income taxes on the money before you invest it; you pay the taxes when you make withdrawals at retirement. Deferred means delayed or postponed; you pay taxes later.

Money contributed to a **Roth IRA is not Tax Deferred.** This means you pay income taxes on the money before you invest it. This money is referred to as after-tax dollars. The growth is tax-free; once you put your money in, you never pay taxes on it again.

READ THE SMALL PRINT AND AVOID FEES

Before investing in a Roth IRA or any other investment, read all the information. If there is something you don't understand, go on-line and do some research. Watch out for fees, and make sure all of your deposits go directly into your account. Avoid startup fees, annual maintenance fees, fees for changing your investments, fees for transferring your account to another company, or fees for withdrawing your money. Never put your money into something you do not fully understand.

BE CONSISTENT AND PERSISTENT

Budget your money so you can continually make the maximum contribution every year. Over time, your money will grow. Remember: The two keys to creating financial wealth are consistency and persistence. Make your money work for you throughout your life.

BECOME A LIFELONG INVESTOR

Everyone, no matter what their age or financial status, should establish a Roth IRA if they qualify. The Roth IRA is a fantastic way for you to save money while benefiting from tax-free growth. The earlier you start investing, the more your investment base will grow. Commit to regular and systematic investing.

ACT NOW

Opening a Roth IRA is simple, easy, and convenient. If you have earned income, you can't afford not to take advantage of the tax benefits a Roth IRA provides. Don't put it off another day. Act now!

A LAURIE STORY

No Drama to Report!

Trust yourself. Think for yourself. Act for yourself. Speak for yourself. Be yourself. Imitation is suicide.

— *Marva Collins*

What's there to say? Not much. I have a Roth IRA and I fund it annually. I always contribute the maximum amount, and I monitor my account to ensure my investment choices are consistent with my financial short and long-term goals. This is one area of my life in which there is no drama to report. Yippee!!!

Money demands that you sell, not your weakness to men's stupidity, but your talent to their reason.

— *Ayn Rand*

Activity

What? It's Mine and It's Tax Free?

Read the following scenario. Then answer the question.

Let's say you're nine years old and you earn money working in your parent's office, or from paid chores around the house. Suppose you invest your earnings in a Roth IRA. You invest it in a mutual fund that doesn't charge fees and has an average 11 percent rate of return.

Flash forward: You're 18 years old and about to graduate from high school. How much do you have? You have about $30,000! Of this $30,000, $18,000 is the money you put in – your contributions over the years. The balance of your account, approximately $12,000, is the money you've earned from your mutual fund investments.

Now you have $30,000. The Roth IRA rules state you can take out your contributions. You can withdraw the $18,000 you put in and you won't be charged a penalty. You don't pay taxes on this money because you already paid the tax on the money before you invested it in your Roth IRA. This is what's called after-tax dollars. Get it? After-Tax?

If you wanted to pay for your college education with the balance of the money, you could withdraw that too. However, if you withdraw the balance before you turn 59 1/2 years old, you will have to pay taxes on it. These earnings represent money on which you have NOT yet paid taxes. They are pre-tax (before tax) dollars.

If you leave the entire $30,000 in your account and don't touch it until you turn 60 years old you will have…drum roll, please…almost $2.7 million dollars! And guess what? It's all yours, tax free!

Not bad, huh?

Are you doing all that you can to build your financial future?

Without leaps of imagination, or dreaming, we lose the excitement of possibilities. Dreaming, after all, is a form of planning.

— Gloria Steinem

PROTECTING YOURSELF FROM IDENTITY THEFT AND FRAUD

I am an optimist. But I am an optimist who takes his raincoat.

— *Sir Harold Wilson.*

Identity theft and fraud are on the rise. They are the fastest growing, non-violent crimes in the US. If you drive, take your trash outside, use a credit or debit card, mail checks, or have a mail box, you're a prime target for identity theft and fraud. Identity theft occurs when a thief steals another person's information and abuses it.

It often starts with the theft of a credit card, checkbook, bank statement, ATM number, license, Social Security number, passport, etc. If a criminal acquires enough of your personal information they can begin their game. They use your name to take out loans, apply for credit cards, withdraw money from your bank accounts, rack up traffic tickets, and more.

These activities cause damage to your credit profile and by the time you find out – it's often too late. Tens or hundreds of thousands of dollars of credit may have been obtained using your name. By then, the collection agencies are calling you to find out why you're overdue. Victims of identify theft spend years and a lot of money to fix these problems. There are simple steps you can take to protect your private information and to reduce the risk of becoming a victim of identity theft.

DON'T TRASH YOUR CREDIT AND YOUR GOOD NAME BY BEING CARELESS,
PROTECT YOUR VALUABLE DOCUMENTS,

☀ RICH CHOICES ☀

Protecting Yourself from Identity Theft and Fraud

- Trash is No Longer Worthless, Shred It
- Guard Your Incoming and Outgoing Mail
- Guard Your Cards From "Shoulder Surfers"
- Eliminate the Paper Chase
- Don't Just Walk Away
- Reduce the Number of Cards You Carry in Your Wallet
- You Make the Call
- Examine the Charges
- Remove Your Name
- Protect Your PIN (Personal Identification Number)
- Safeguard Your Social Security Number
- Leave Your Checkbook Home

TRASH IS NO LONGER WORTHLESS, SHRED IT

Thieves engage in "dumpster diving." That's when someone goes through your trash looking for copies of your checks, credit cards, bank statements, or other records. These types of records make it easy for them to access accounts in your name and assume your identity. Don't simply throw away account statements, junk mail, old checks, and bank statements. Get a shredder and use it. Shred everything that contains identifying information on it. Today, the trash is the greatest repository of information for the identity thief.

GUARD YOUR INCOMING AND OUTGOING MAIL

Thieves steal incoming and outgoing mail. They obtain your personal information and account numbers and start using your credit. Drop your outgoing mail at the Post Office, into mailboxes that are locked, or at a secure workplace. Don't leave your mail out overnight. The same goes for your home mailbox. Put a lock on your box or get a Post Office box. If you're going to be away from home for any length of time, have your newspapers and home delivery stopped.

GUARD YOUR CARDS FROM "SHOULDER SURFERS"

At restaurants, retail stores, ATM's, and any other places you do business, be aware of people standing close to you who may be "shoulder surfing." Watch out for individuals holding camera cell phones who may take pictures of your card. This provides them with your name, number, and expiration date. Then they can spend, spend, and spends some more – all on your dime!

ELIMINATE THE PAPER CHASE

The more accounts you have the more paperwork you have to manage. Extra paperwork increases your chances of a thief stealing your records from your mailbox or trash can. If you have credit cards that you're not using, lock them in a strong box or other safe place. Close unnecessary accounts.

DON'T JUST WALK AWAY

When paying for gas at the pump, or completing a transaction at the ATM, don't leave receipts that may contain your personal information. Be sure to collect and protect all your charge card and ATM receipts. Dispose of them on your own.

REDUCE THE NUMBER OF CARDS YOU CARRY IN YOUR WALLET

You don't need to carry an excessive amount of credit cards in your wallet. If your wallet is lost or stolen, think of the number of creditors you will have to contact. Carrying extra cards for department stores and service stations is dangerous and unnecessary. Consider using just one or two cards for all your purchases.

YOU MAKE THE CALL

Never, ever give your Social Security number, account number, PIN (Personal Identification Number), or other personal data over the phone or on-line unless you initiated the contact. A criminal may call you pretending to be a bank employee or someone from your credit card company. Don't give out any personal information over the phone. If necessary, hang up and call the company yourself. This way you'll know the contact is legitimate.

EXAMINE THE CHARGES

When you receive your credit card and banking statements, examine them carefully for suspicious activity. Always verify that all checks and charges are accurate prior to making payments or filing paperwork. Reconcile your bank statements as soon as you receive them.

Remove Your Name

Remove your name from the marketing lists of the three credit reporting bureaus to reduce the number of pre-approved credit offers you receive in the mail. Dial 1-888-5OPT-OUT to stop credit bureaus from selling your name to credit card companies.

Protect Your PIN (Personal Identification Number)

Our society is moving towards a cashless system of transactions. As a result, we use more PIN's to complete various transactions. Do not write your PIN on your ATM or debit card or have it anywhere in your wallet or checkbook. Don't leave your PIN and your cards in the same location, even at home. Keep them in a separate place.

Safeguard Your Social Security Number

Your Social Security number is the key to your credit report and bank accounts. It's the main item a criminal needs. Do not carry your Social Security card with you. Do not print your Social Security number on your checks. Don't be careless with your personal information. Should you become a victim of fraud, as millions of Americans are today, you will go through unbelievable torture to get your life straightened out again.

Leave Your Checkbook Home

If lost or stolen it could spell disaster, especially since most check fraud starts with the theft of a check. Information like your phone number, Social Security number, and home address should not be on your personal checks and driver's license. Consider using only your last name and your first initial rather than your full name on your checks. Eliminate your middle initial as well. Using your middle initial helps a thief narrow down their search for victims. Keep your checks in a safe place.

If you become a victim of identity theft or fraud, here's what you need to do:

- File a police report and make sure you receive a copy. If you can't get a copy, get the report number. This is critical.

- If your credit card has been compromised, cancel the card by reporting it lost or stolen to your credit card company immediately.

- Complete affidavits with all financial institutions with whom you do business.

- Report the fraud to the three major credit bureaus.

> *Although the world is full of suffering, it is also full of the overcoming of it.*
>
> — *Helen Keller*

A LAURIE STORY

I Do What I Can to Protect My SSN!

> *The trouble with most people is that they think with their hopes or fears or wishes rather than with their minds.*
>
> — *Lady Nancy Astor*

Identity theft has reached epidemic proportions. An estimated 13 million American consumers were victims of identity theft in 2004. Fortunately, I was not among them. I am very careful with my personal information. Whenever I am asked to provide my Social Security number, I am always very hesitant. I ask a lot of questions and my bottom line is always: "Is there an alternative form of identifying information I can provide?"

In addition to containing your credit score, your credit report contains your Social Security number. Whenever I apply for a credit card, a car, automobile insurance, a job, or anything else, my credit report is always checked. I am very protective of my Social Security number. At the completion of every application process, I tell the person handling my application that I want my Social Security number truncated or completely erased from my application. I do this because I don't want to leave my personal information in the hands of someone I don't know.

I also request that my original credit report be shredded (while I watch) or returned to me once a decision has been made. A lender, rental manager, or anyone else making a decision about my application only needs to keep my name and credit score to make the decision. To some people this may seem excessive; I don't care if I annoy the person handling my application. This is what I do to protect my Social Security number.

> *Money is the most important thing in the world. It represents health, strength, honor, generosity and beauty as conspicuously as the want of it represents illness, weakness, disgrace, meanness and ugliness.*
>
> — *George Bernard Shaw*

Activity

Where are Your V.I.P.'s (Very Important Paper's)?

Do you toss receipts or other important papers into a shoe box or drawer? Maintaining an orderly record keeping system is one of the best ways to protect your good name from identity theft and fraud. Being organized with your V.I.P.'s can save you lots of time and money.

How organized are you with your **V.I.P.'s**?

Answer 'Yes' or 'No' to the following questions:
Can you quickly locate your bank statements? _____
Do you know where your original Social Security card is? _____
Do you keep all your receipts in one place in an organized fashion?
_____
Do you have the account numbers, addresses, and phone numbers of all your credit cards companies handy? _____
Could a non-family member locate important information, on your behalf, in case of an emergency? _____
Can you locate the warranties, receipts, and other paperwork for all your electronic and computer purchases? _____
If you have filed a tax return, can you locate it quickly? _____

If you answered "No" to one or more of these questions, it's time to make changes in your record keeping habits – NOW! Organizing paperwork may not be the most pleasurable thing to do, but it is very necessary. Tossing old papers into a shoebox or a drawer just isn't good enough.

Create an organized record keeping system that is effective, efficient, and that works for you. Commit to being purposeful and business-wise about your personal affairs. Have a certain place you always keep certain items. It pays great dividends!

> *Become a person who neither looks up to the rich or down on the poor…take your share of the world and let other people have theirs.*
>
> — *George Washington Carver*

LIFE COMMITMENTS

I'M COMMITTED TO:

- Always doing my best
- Setting meaningful short and long-term goals
- Sacrificing to achieve my goals – not putting today's wants before tomorrow's needs
- Exercising good judgment and maintaining positive thoughts
- Intelligently managing my time, my energy, and my resources
- Letting go of the small, petty, insignificant stuff
- Never accepting "No" from someone who doesn't have the authority to say "Yes"
- Running with the big dogs and associating with positive, "GROWTH" people
- Designing my life with passion
- Appreciating all my talents, gifts, and uniqueness

X_____   _____
Sign Here   Date

FINANCIAL COMMITMENTS

I'M COMMITTED TO:

- Paying myself first
- Monitoring and controlling my spending
- Spending less than I earn
- Establishing long-term savings
- Respecting small amounts of money
- Keeping debts and liabilities to a minimum
- Paying my bills in full, before the due date, avoiding all late fees and finance charges
- Balancing my checkbook regularly
- Setting financial goals and assessing them often
- Investing early, investing regularly, and investing systematically
- Protecting myself against identity theft and fraud
- Monitoring my credit report and my credit rating regularly
- Becoming financially literate and managing my economic future
- Giving generously of my time, my money, and my talents

X_____   _____
Sign Here   Date

STOP DREAMING! DECIDE WHAT YOU WANT AND...

Work passionately to achieve your goals.

Act with love in all you do.

Keep moving and remain focused.

Eliminate self-defeating thoughts and habits.

Understand that choice, not chance determines your future.

Persist until you succeed.

Commit to Making Rich Choices!